chicken

THE NEW CLASSICS

chicken

THE NEW CLASSICS

Marcus Bean

NOURISH

EAT WELL, LIVE WELL

DEDICATION
For Jenny, Ella and Ava. And for all the
chickens out there being used in rubbish
recipes—it's time to cook you properly!

Chicken
Marcus Bean

First published in the USA and Canada in 2014
by Nourish, an imprint of
Watkins Publishing Limited
PO Box 883
Oxford, OX1 9PL,
UK

A member of Osprey Group

Osprey Publishing
PO Box 3985
New York, NY 10185-3985
Tel: (001) 212 753 4402
Email: info@ospreypublishing.com

Copyright © Watkins Publishing Limited 2014
Text and recipes copyright © Marcus Bean 2014
Artwork copyright © Watkins Publishing Limited 2014
Photography copyright © Watkins Publishing Limited 2014

The right of Marcus Bean to be identified as the Author of
this text has been asserted in accordance with the Copyright,
Designs and Patents Act of 1988.

All rights reserved. No part of this book may be reproduced in
any form or by any electronic or mechanical means, including
information storage and retrieval systems, without permission
in writing from the publisher, except by a reviewer who may
quote brief passages in a review.

Publisher: Grace Cheetham
Project Editor: Rebecca Woods
Editor: Wendy Hobson
Designer: Manisha Patel
Production: Uzma Taj
Commissioned photography: Martin Poole,
except for page 7, Victoria Macken
Food Stylist: Aya Nishimura
Prop Stylist: Wei Tang
Americanizer: Delora Jones

ISBN: 978-1-84899-197-2

10 9 8 7 6 5 4 3 2 1

Typeset in Filosofia
Color reproduction by PDQ, UK
Printed in China

Publisher's note
While every care has been taken in compiling the recipes for
this book, Watkins Publishing Limited, or any other persons
who have been involved in working on this publication, cannot
accept responsibility for any errors or omissions, inadvertent
or not, that may be found in the recipes or text, nor for any
problems that may arise as a result of preparing one of these
recipes. If you are pregnant or breastfeeding or have any
special dietary requirements or medical conditions, it is
advisable to consult a medical professional before following
any of the recipes contained in this book. Ill or elderly people,
babies, young children, and women who are pregnant or
breastfeeding should avoid recipes containing raw meat or
fish or uncooked eggs.

Notes on the recipes
Unless otherwise stated:
· Use cage-free eggs and cage-free poultry
· Use medium eggs, fruit and vegetables
· Use fresh ingredients, including herbs and chilies
· 1 teaspoon = 5ml 1 tablespoon = 15ml 1 cup = 240ml

Watkins Publishing Limited is supporting the Woodland Trust,
the UK's leading woodland conservation charity, by funding
tree-planting initiatives and woodland maintenance.

nourishbooks.com

contents

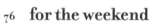

introduction

Always one of my favorite ingredients, chicken is succulent, flavorsome, versatile, inexpensive and healthy. It's very popular in our house as my wife, Jenny, hasn't eaten red meat since she was a child, so I've cooked more chicken than most, but we never get fed up with it—why should we? Few foods blend as well with such a range of different ingredients and flavorings, so there's always something different to try. In fact, I can't think of anything that couldn't be successfully paired with chicken to make a delicious meal—from delicate to robust foods, from subtle, creamy sauces to hot fiery curries, fruit or vegetables, fish or cheese, herbs, spices or nuts, rices, legumes or pasta. Plus, as there are mouth-watering chicken dishes in every cuisine around the world—from curries to Oriental stir-fries or chicken and french fries—the sky's the limit.

For a modern and health-conscious diet, too, chicken checks all the boxes as it is both low in fat and a great source of protein. A 3½-ounce serving of baked chicken breast contains 4g of fat and 31g of protein, compared with 10g of fat and 27g of protein for the same portion of broiled lean steak. This makes it a sensible and nutritious part of a healthy balanced diet, and great for those who are trying to slim down a little, too—cooked in the right way, of course.

Chicken is also fantastically versatile. It can be cooked by almost any cooking method—slowly for a succulent stew, or quickly with a crisp, pan-fried skin. The various cuts lend themselves to every different style of cooking, giving us so many choices that we can keep the interest going in our meals—even if we were to eat chicken every day.

As well as its versatility, in these budget-conscious times, chicken scores highly as an inexpensive meat. And the fact that nothing is wasted—even the carcass makes wonderful soup or stock—is an added bonus. It's hard to think of a better set of credentials for any ingredient to be chosen as the star of a book and I hope you'll enjoy seeing it in the spotlight.

So I am delighted to be able to share some of my favorite chicken recipes with you. In writing this book, I set out to discover as much as I could about chicken and why we love it so much, and I have created recipes that I hope will inspire you to experiment and enjoy this fabulous meat as much as I do. I have set out to give you the best of the classic chicken recipes, experimenting with modern and unexpected twists along the way. But I have also created new recipes, exploring great flavor combinations that I hope will help you to revolutionize the way you cook with chicken.

THE ICONIC RECIPES

Because of chicken's versatility, cooks around the world have all taken chicken into their kitchens and created some of the most delicious recipes, each one with that perfect balance of ingredients. Some are recognized pairings, others evolved from happy accident resulting in flavors, textures, colors and cooking methods that make a really classic dish. These dishes have stood the test of time, and some of them are a starting point for my own recipes in this book.

Coq au vin was one of the first dishes I mastered as a chef, and I had to include a classic version (see page 110) because it is a recipe that still fits perfectly into our modern lifestyle. "Cockerel with wine" is known by every chef around the world. Based on the classic principles of French cuisine, this slow braise of chicken in red wine with mushrooms, bacon lardons and garlic makes a rich and warming dish. Created in the early twentieth century, its popularity was assured by the TV chef Julia Child, who featured the dish on her TV show and in the breakthrough 1961 cookbook, co-written with S. Beck and L. Bertholle, *Mastering the Art of French Cooking*.

Another recipe that I just had to include was a version of Caesar salad. In the 1920s, the Italian immigrant restaurateur, Caesar Cardini, was running a successful business in the US and Mexico. The story goes that after a rush in one of his restaurants, he would take all the ingredients he had left in the kitchen tableside and create a salad for the customer. Caesar salad emerged from that imaginative blending of ingredients: romaine lettuce, croutons, parmesan cheese, lemon juice, olive oil, egg, Worcestershire sauce, garlic and black pepper. Cooks have continued to experiment, adapt and tweak it in an infinite number of ways, including adding chicken to the recipe, and I have carried on that tradition. My modern version takes each element individually so they can shine in their own right. I hope you will enjoy my Deconstructed Crisp Pancetta & Charred-lettuce Caesar Salad with Anchovy Straws (see page 141).

I've always loved chicken Kiev—a dish of battered chicken wrapped around cold garlic butter, bread crumbed and fried to a golden and crisp finish. Traditionally considered Ukrainian in origin—hardly surprising since Kiev is the capital of Ukraine—the Russian food historian William Pokhlebkin insists that it was invented in the Moscow Merchants' Club in the early twentieth century, and was later renamed chicken Kiev when it was marketed for restaurants in Europe. I have taken it to another continent in my Asian-Style Chicken Kiev (see page 188) to give it a whole new dimension.

Another recent classic, fajitas—or "little meat"—became popular in the 1990s, spreading around the world from its home in Mexican and American restaurants with its characteristic sizzle. So often, we reach for the ready-made options when we enjoy this dish with family and friends, but I hope my Chicken Fajitas & Homemade Smoked Paprika Wraps (see page 42) will encourage you to make it all from scratch. It's easier than you'd think.

Back home in the UK, I had to include that British classic, roast chicken. I fondly remember growing up in an English pub, run by my parents, and how we used to gather on Sunday for a family meal of roast chicken, often with as many as eight extra guests—usually friends of mine invited at the last minute. Even though the popularity of the traditional Sunday roast is waning as our lifestyles change, roast chicken still appears regularly on lunch and dinner tables—and not only on Sundays—accompanied by roast potatoes, vegetables and gravy (although serving Yorkshire pudding remains contentious, many people insisting that it only goes with beef). When I roast chicken, I always know it is going to be tender and succulent because I soak it in brine before cooking. Try Lemon Verbena & Thyme-roasted Chicken (see page 132) and you'll see what I mean.

CHICKEN BREEDS

So let's take a step back to find out a little about these valuable birds. Around 5,000 years ago in Asia, the red jungle fowl gradually gave rise to the modern chicken, which is now one of the most common and widespread domestic animals in the world. Estimates suggest that the worldwide chicken population is well over 24 billion (although I have no idea who counts them all!). That means there are more chickens in the world than any other species of bird. More than 50 billion chickens are reared annually as a source of food, and we eat both their meat and their eggs. In the UK alone, with a population roughly one-fifth that of the US, we consume more than 29 million eggs every day, so it's a good thing that some breeds of hen can produce over 300 eggs per year, the record being a somewhat surprising 371 eggs.

There are hundreds of different breeds of chicken around the world, and even more crossbreeds, each with its own characteristics defined in terms of its place of origin, size, plumage and color. Generally speaking, each breed is better for producing either eggs or meat, although some breeds are considered dual purpose. Farmers or individuals, therefore, have plenty of choice to select the breed that will give them the best results, depending on their circumstances and whether they want prolific egg-layers or particular flavors of meat.

Among the most valued egg-layers are the Rhode Island Red, the New Hampshire Red and the Australorp. These breeds all have the added advantage that they are good foragers and don't fly well, making it easier to keep them safely in a farmyard or garden. The Australorp is particularly noted for its docile temperament, another reason why it is a good hen for beginners.

One of the most notable breeds for meat is the French Poulet de Bresse, which produces such a high-quality product that it is sought after by chefs all over the world, while the French chefs endeavour to use most of it at home. Popular dual-purpose birds include the Orpington, the Plymouth Rock—a particularly good choice for those in colder areas, and the Sussex.

And that's just the hens. There are also the roosters—called cocks in the UK and Ireland, or cockerels if they are less than a year old. The meat from a rooster tends to be slightly tougher but is great for stocks, broths and slow-cooked stews, as are stewing chicken, which are over ten months old. A spring chicken—known as a poussin in the UK—is a smaller bird, ideal for individual servings.

As I write, we have three young roosters that roam around weeding the flower beds for us. We keep our hens at my mother-in-law's as she tends all the chickens to supply us with eggs and meat. We use them for our B & B, our cooking school and, of course, for our own breakfast every day. Our plan is to keep more hens at home very soon.

INTENSIVE FARMING & ORGANIC FARMING
Until the middle of the twentieth century, chicken was regarded as a luxury and graced the tables only on special occasions. It was the advent of intensive rearing methods that changed its status, making chicken both plentiful and inexpensive, and it is now the most commonly eaten meat around the world.

Of course, that came with disadvantages—not least for the chickens—including overcrowding, poor health and being kept constantly caged. Non-cage-free birds feed on grain coated with antibiotics to improve their resistance to disease, while living in cramped conditions. The meat is often bland and tasteless, and is sometimes pumped with water to make it more tender

Adverse reaction to intensive poultry farming has led to the resurgence of the old ways, and many people—including me—seek out both eggs and meat from organic and cage-free chickens because the way the chicken is raised affects both the

quality of the meat and also the quality of the eggs—quite apart from any ethical considerations. The regulations are complex, but the main difference between a cage-free and a cage-free organic bird is that the organic birds are not routinely fed antibiotics or artificial supplements to maintain their general health.

Both cage-free and organic birds are fed corn mix and are allowed to roam outside in the daytime in the fields or open spaces and forage for feed such as insects, worms, clover, herbs or flowers. This means they have a more natural and varied diet, which adds both flavor to the meat and also improves the quality, color and flavor of the eggs.

The relaxed environment also allows them to develop in their own time, being given about 14 weeks to mature, while intensively farmed chickens are slaughtered at six weeks. As the cage-free birds can roam the farmyard, the chickens build stronger muscles in both the legs and breast, giving the meat a firmer texture as well as more intense flavor. That is why my favorite way to cook chicken legs is to cook them slowly and gently in oil to make a confit, or in a stew to break down the muscle until it is so tender it simply falls off the bone.

RAISING CHICKENS AT HOME

Many people raise their own hens, which is not difficult in an ordinary yard since all you need is a small amount of land and enough room for a cage and an open-air run. Although they certainly can't fly very high or very far, you must not forget that domestic chickens are not completely flightless, although their skills in this department do vary considerably. Some breeds, especially the lighter birds, can fly short distances, such as over fences or into trees (where they would naturally roost), so you can make it easier if you choose breeds that are poor flyers.

Incidentally, egg-laying hens do not need males to produce eggs, only to fertilize them, so an all-female flock will still produce eggs for you, even though the eggs will all be infertile.

Whatever you choose, I'm sure you'll get as much enjoyment out of keeping chickens as we do. Apart from the eggs and meat, they are such lovely creatures to have around. I know several people who have been worn down by their family's enthusiasm and only reluctantly agreed to keep chickens, but who have since become their strongest advocate. I love going out in the morning and bringing back a basket of the freshest of eggs for our breakfast, cracking them into a pan to reveal their bright yolks, then enjoying the rich, creamy flavor.

buying chicken

When it comes to buying chicken, my preference is for a good cage-free, preferably organic, bird because, as we have seen, this gives a superior flavor and texture to both the eggs and the meat. My favorite place to buy a chicken would always be right from the farmer or from a farmers' market, because you can see how the chickens are reared and talk to the people who tend them. You get a real sense of where your food is coming from and I try and do this with all the meat and vegetables I buy. It also helps to inspire me to create new recipe ideas. You may have a local butcher or farmers' market near you, but many supermarkets also stock superior-quality products. In addition, the internet now gives you access to great-quality cage-free and organic chicken right from the farms and delivered to your door, so no one needs to miss out on great-quality meat.

A good supplier will keep their meat in a cooler at the correct temperature, well wrapped and with an appropriate use-by date. If it has already been frozen, that should be indicated as you should not refreeze chicken once it has thawed. The birds should be plump and firm, with white, unbroken skin, or yellow for a corn-fed chicken. If you have sensibly left your meat shopping until last, the meat will spend the shortest amount of time out of the refrigerator.

CUTS OF CHICKEN

A good supplier will offer whole birds, which usually work out cheaper, or a variety of cuts. If you buy from a butcher, you can buy a whole chicken and ask for it to be prepared in any way you want so you have one less thing to think about before you start cooking. Most butchers will bone your chicken thighs to save you time, and even give you free carcasses for stock. Just ask! They normally give them to restaurants or dispose of them. Once you've made the stock you can freeze it down in batches to keep until you need it (see page 197).

Whole

An average chicken weighs about 3 pounds 2 ounces to 4 pounds but larger birds can weigh up to 6 pounds. The simplest way to cook a whole chicken is to roast it just with a touch of seasoning, but I like to soak it in an herb-infused brine before I cook it to make sure it is extra moist and succulent (see page 17).

Half

A half-chicken has been cut through the center of the breast with a pair of heavy kitchen scissors or poultry shears, removing the spine in the process. Half-chickens can also be roasted but are great on the barbecue or under the broiler, too, especially when the skin is rubbed with spices

Supreme, statler or airline breast

More common in the UK than the US, this is the breast with the wing attached and weighs about 7 ounces. By leaving the wing on, it allows the breast to retain a little more moisture, although the choice of serving chicken supremes is mainly one of presentation as they look good on the plate. They are most often pan-fried, but can otherwise be cooked in the same ways as the breast, and you can substitute breast in any of the recipes if you can find statler breasts. One of my favorite recipes is Crisp-Skinned Chicken with Sweet Potato Puree, Kale & Crisp Leeks (see page 127), a colorful dish with loads of contrasting textures.

Breast

Breasts are white meat with no bone, usually weighing 4½ to 8 ounces. Great whole or cubed for every kind of cooking method, from pan-frying and broiling to poaching, stews and stir-fries, they are quick to cook but can tend to dry out if overcooked. Using a digital meat thermometer will help you avoid this. Check the internal temperature when you think the chicken is ready, then let it rest for a few minutes after cooking to allow the meat to relax. If you are frying, cook with the skin on as this also helps to keep the meat moist.

Cuts of chicken
1 Thighs
2 Drumsticks
3 Fillets
4 Breast
5 Supreme (statler breast)
6 Drumette
7 Middle and tip of wings

Wings

Often served as a snack, the wings offer a good flavor with a mixture of light and dark meat. They fry or roast well and are cooked with the skin on. There are three segments to the wings: the drumette is shaped like a small drumstick; the middle, flat segment contains two bones; and the tip is generally discarded as it has little meat on it, although you can put it in with your meat and bones for stock.

Leg

The whole leg can be sold as a cut, or divided into the thigh, the upper part, and the drumstick. Both are dark meat, which generally has more a lot more flavor than the breast and is moister in texture. The meat can be fried, roasted, poached or broiled, or it can be slow-cooked in stews. The thigh meat particularly loves to be slow cooked until tender and falling apart. Legs can be cooked with or without the skin, and can be boned before cooking, either to make them easier to eat, or to use for stuffing. The drumsticks make great quick snack food.

Giblets

It's a shame that most people tend to throw away the giblets—the little bundle of parts sometimes found inside the cavity of a bird. They usually include the neck, the gizzard (a muscle that grinds up food before it enters the digestive system), the heart and the liver. I like to use the giblets to make a stock, which I add to the pan after I've roasted a chicken to make a fabulous gravy. You could try that yourself, or add them to my Chicken Broth recipe for extra flavor (see page 197), then use that stock to make your gravy.

Liver

The liver is the largest organ of the chicken and is often sold separately. It is generally used in pâtés and terrines, or simply pan-fried in butter. The texture is very light and delicate, and it goes really well with rich foods like cream and butter, and also strong flavors like smoked bacon and herbs. Sometimes there's nothing better than a good spread of rich, smooth, homemade chicken liver pâté on hot toast with butter. Try my version, Chicken Liver & Sweet Wine Jelly Pâté for the perfect treat (see page 152).

Carcass

After the removal of the flesh, the bones and remaining attached meat can be used for making soups and stock (see page 197). Your local butcher may just give you some spare carcasses—otherwise they normally give them to restaurants or just dispose of them.

STORING CHICKEN

Everyone knows that you have to be careful with chicken and make sure you handle and store it correctly because, if you don't, it can be prone to developing harmful bacteria. Having said that, if you follow a few common-sense rules, you won't have any problems. But because I want you to enjoy your chicken, here's just a quick reminder how to treat it.

You should always keep raw or cooked chicken in the refrigerator, which should be at or below 37 to 41°F. If you are not sure whether your refrigerator is working efficiently, you can buy—or, better still, borrow—a refrigerator thermometer. The place for raw meat is at the bottom of the refrigerator so there is no chance it will drip onto other food. Store any cooked meat separately at the top of the refrigerator. Both raw and cooked chicken can be stored in the refrigerator for about 4 days, but do keep an eye on the use-by date and follow your instinct—if you are not happy that the meat still looks and smells fresh, then don't use it.

Your meat may already be packaged when you buy it, but if not, wrap it in plastic wrap and put it on a plate to collect any inevitable drips. To make sure it is well sealed, I use a vacuum sealer, which removes all the air and seals the chicken in a bag. You can buy small versions that are great for using at home—and you can use them for wrapping all sorts of foods for the refrigerator or the freezer, so they have loads more uses than just wrapping chicken. Once refrigerated, meat that you have vacuum-packed will stay fresh for twice as long as meat wrapped in plastic wrap or just in a plastic bag, so it is also much more hygienic.

If you want to freeze chicken, I always recommend that you buy the chicken fresh, make sure it is properly wrapped, then label and freeze it yourself. However, if you do buy frozen chicken, make sure you get it back in the freezer as quickly as possible so it does not start to defrost. Freezers should run at -4°F or colder and you can keep meat frozen almost indefinitely, although up to three months is recommended for the best flavor and texture.

Allow plenty of time to defrost your chicken before you cook it. Remove it from the freezer, place it on a tray in the refrigerator and let it defrost slowly over about 24 hours. Once fully thawed, cook it within 24 hours. It is possible to cook smaller cuts right from frozen but you just need to be aware that it will take at least twice as long to cook as unfrozen chicken, and you must ensure that you cook it through thoroughly, preferably using a digital thermometer to check its cooked temperature. Once thawed, don't refreeze chicken.

preparing chicken

You may want to ask your butcher to prepare your chicken, or simply buy ready-prepared meat, but it is more economical to buy a whole chicken to cut up and prepare, so why not have a try. You will find that, with a little practice, it will soon become second nature. It is really important to have at least one good-quality knife in the kitchen. A sharp knife will make a massive difference to your cooking, from chopping to crushing to filleting.

Just as with proper storage rules, remember a few common-sense hygiene rules when you are preparing chicken. There's no need to wash chicken before you cook it. In fact, the nasty microbes or bacteria are destroyed by proper cooking, whereas you are much more likely to spread them around the kitchen if you are trying to wash the bird in the sink. Keep other ingredients out of the way while you get your chicken ready, so there are fewer chances of cross-contamination, especially with raw foods. Don't answer the phone if it rings while you are cutting up a bird, or rake through the knife drawer. Concentrate on the chicken, then clear up all your working tools, knives and so on. Wash your hands, all your counters and your utensils with antibacterial hand wash or cleaner, then dry them with paper towels.

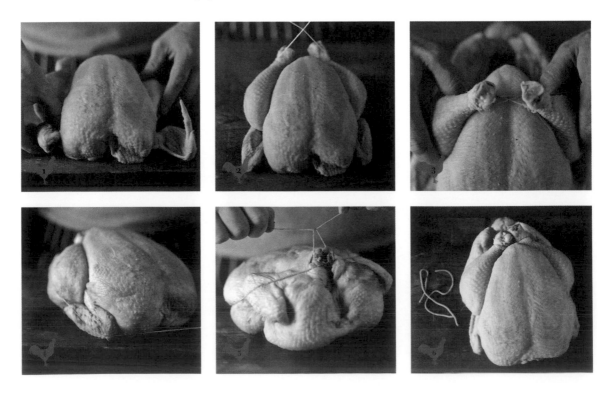

TRUSSING A BIRD FOR ROASTING

If you like, you can secure a bird neatly with string, using a ball of kitchen twine. Some cooks feel it helps the chicken cook more evenly, others disagree. For normal roasting, it is a matter of choice. However, if you are cooking the chicken on a barbecue, or especially a rotisserie, where it is going to be turned frequently, it is a good idea to truss since it keeps the bird neatly together and makes cooking much easier. You can also truss a bird for brining.

1 Place the bird on its back and fold the tip of the wings in under the bird so they are tucked in snugly.
2 Take some kitchen twine and run it under the legs. Cross the string over the top, then wrap each end of the string under the opposite leg.
3 Pull the string tight to pull the legs together firmly.
4 Run the strings around the sides of the chicken, making sure it goes over the wings and thighs, to hold them in position.
5 Turn the chicken over and tie the ends of the string together under the base of the neck bone.
6 The trussed chicken is now ready for roasting.

BRINING

Brining is soaking chicken in salted water before roasting or smoking in order to keep the meat moist when it is cooking or being smoked. You can brine chicken for any of the recipes in this book.

FOR THE BRINE:
1 cup salt
2 large lemon verbena sprigs
1 carrot, peeled and cut in half
1 garlic bulb, cut in half horizontally
scant 1/2 cup light soy sauce
2 large thyme sprigs
1 onion, cut in half

Dissolve the brine ingredients in about 6 quarts water. Add the chicken, making sure it is covered in the brine. Cover and leave in the refrigerator overnight, or for about 12 hours. Drain well, rinse, then drain again before cooking.

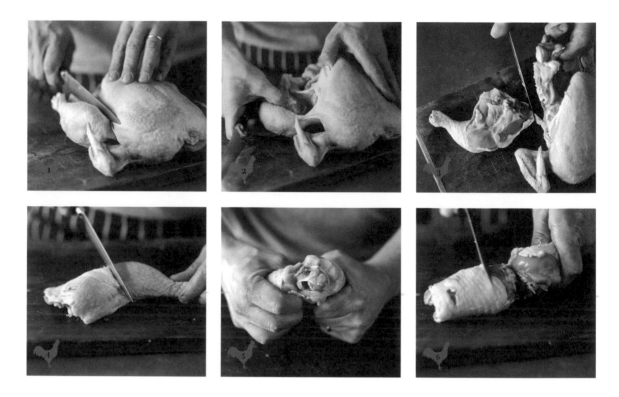

CUTTING UP A CHICKEN

1 Set the chicken on a secure cutting board and cut off any trussing string. Using a sharp knife, slit the skin between the thigh and the breast and move the leg away from the body so that you can see the joint.

2 Pull the leg fully away from the body and the leg joint will pop out.

3 Run the knife through the joint to separate the leg. Repeat with the other leg. This will give you the two legs, each with the drumstick and the thigh together.

4 To separate the thigh and the drumstick, put the leg on the cutting board and run your finger down the drumstick until you can feel the joint. Slice through the skin at the joint.

5 Hold the leg firmly at either end, then bend the leg in half to break the leg into two at the joint.

6 If you need to, use the knife to finish separating the two pieces by cutting through at the joint.

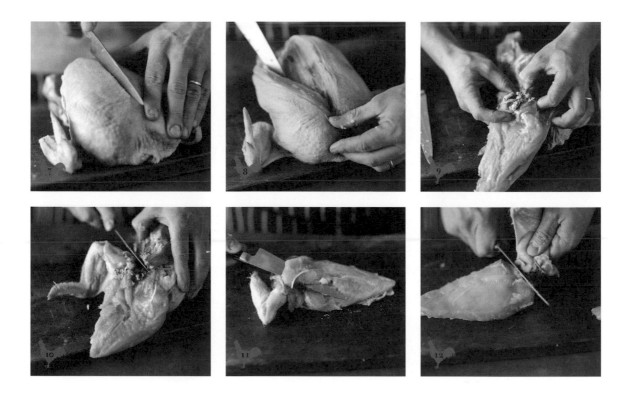

7 Smooth the skin over the breast. Using a small knife, run the knife along the
   wishbone, then slip your fingers under the bone and snap it out in two pieces
   to make it easier to cut away the breast. To remove the supreme (the breast and
   wing), slowly run a sharp knife along the breastbone.
8 Gradually run the knife down against the inner bone to allow the breast to
   come away from the carcass.
9 The chicken breast will still be attached at the bottom by the wing. Slowly pop
   the wing out of the socket.
10 Run your knife around the breast to release the supreme.
11 The fillets are the small, loose pieces of flesh on the under side of the breast.
   Simply slice these away with a knife, if necessary.
12 If you only want the breast, slowly cut around the base of the wing to release
   and debone the breast. Keep the carcass and trimmings for making stock.

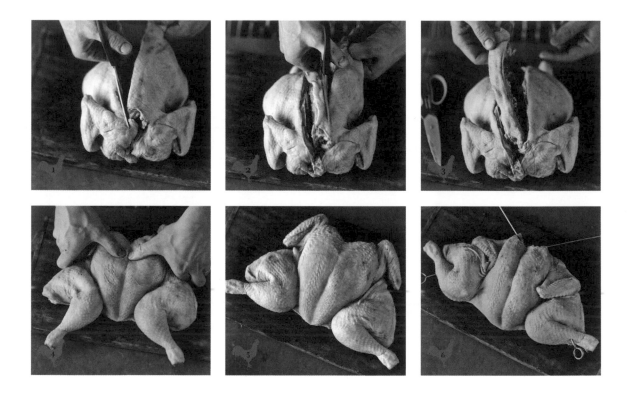

SPATCHCOCKING A BIRD

1 Place the bird on its breast and, using a pair of sharp kitchen shears, cut down along one side of the back bone.

2 Cut down along the other side of the back bone in the same way.

3 Remove the back bone.

4 Turn the chicken over and slowly push down on the breast to flatten the bird.

5 The chicken is now ready for cooking.

6 If you wish, you can insert 2 skewers diagonally through the bird, which will hold the chicken in place and conduct the heat through the thickest part of the chicken, making it cook more quickly and evenly.

 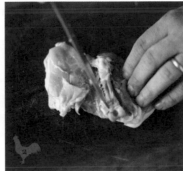 

BONING A THIGH

1 Place the thigh on the cutting board, then turn it over so that the skin is underneath.
2 Using a sharp knife, cut along the bone to release the flesh.
3 Deepen the cut, running your knife along the bone, then pull the bone away from the thigh, cutting it free as you do so.

TUNNEL BONING A LEG

1 Grasp the leg by the drumstick joint and use a sharp knife to cut around the top of the leg to release all the tendons.
2 Taking the drumstick in one hand and the thigh in the other, bend the leg right back until you hear the joint break and the bones are separated.
3 Grasp the end of the drumstick bone and pull it all the way through the drumstick meat to remove it, leaving a hollow through the center. Remove the thigh bone in the same way, making sure that you remove all of the material around the joint as you do so.

cooking chicken

The trick with cooking chicken is to match the right technique with the right cut. For example, the breast is perfect for quick cooking methods like frying, while the legs really benefit from slow cooking to break down the muscle and allow the meat to become tender and fall off the bone. Whichever method you choose, chicken must always be thoroughly cooked to the right temperature before serving. Test the meat by using a temperature probe to check that it has reached a core temperature of 170°F, or by pushing a skewer or the tip of a sharp knife into the thickest part to check that the juices run clear, not pink. But avoid piercing the meat until you are pretty sure it is ready, otherwise you will let the precious juices drain out. Once cooked, let the meat relax for just a few minutes and you will find that the meat is much more succulent and tender.

PAN-FRYING

In our busy lives, we often need something that will cook quickly, so pan-fried chicken is a great option. Melt a little butter or oil in a heavy skillet over medium to high heat and, when it is hot and bubbling, add the chicken. Cook it skin-side down first to give a crisp skin and help to seal in moisture. I like to fry it until the chicken is colored and sealed, then finish it in a hot oven, but you can simply cook in the pan until the meat is tender.

This method is best for breast meat and imparts a lovely color and texture to the chicken. You can cook the breasts whole, in which case this is one of the best ways to get a lovely crisp skin, or slice the meat into strips for stir-frying quickly over high heat. Halfway between frying and broiling, if you use a ridged pan to cook chicken, you'll get attractive dark bars across the meat.

BROILING

Like frying, broiling cooks the meat quickly under a direct heat. Heat the broiler, season the meat with salt and pepper and put it on the broiler pan. The burst of heat will seal the outside of the meat, retaining the juices inside, then continue to cook until the meat is cooked through, turning it as necessary. Because there is no additional oil, this is thought to be a slightly healthier option than frying. You can broil any cut of chicken, just make sure the heat is not too high that it overcooks the outside before the meat is cooked through on the inside.

BARBECUE

I love cooking any cuts of chicken on a barbecue, with the extra smoky flavor it imparts. Those with a gas barbecue can add a few smoking chips onto the grill and close the lid for a couple of minutes for similar results.

HOT & COLD SMOKING

A subtle smoky texture is imparted by smoking chicken meat. If you don't have a counter-top smoker, like mine, use a heavy pot and a steamer with a tight-fitting lid. Line the pot with aluminum foil and a layer of wood chips, sit the steamer on top and put your chicken breast on a heatproof plate inside , then seal tightly and smoke the meat over low heat for 20 to 25 minutes. This smoking method doesn't actually cook the meat but adds the flavor of the smoking ingredients, so remember that cold-smoked chicken products still need to be cooked.

ROASTING

Whole chickens or bigger cuts come into their own when roasting. They are sometimes cooked quickly at a higher temperature, or they can be sealed first at a high temperature, then finish cooking at a lower temperature. This combination again achieves the ideal option of crisp skin and moist and tender meat.

SLOW COOKING

Slow cooking chicken in the oven or on the stove almost guarantees succulent results, and slow-cooked stews give superb results, especially for leg and thigh meat, because the long cooking time allows the meat to break down gradually and tenderize while merging with the flavors of the sauce ingredients. You can also slow cook the leg meat in oil.

POACHING & STEAMING

Also on the stove, you can poach chicken in milk, stock or water, bringing the poaching liquid to a boil, then reducing it to a gentle simmer. It is ideal for any type or cut of chicken, although especially good for keeping breast meat moist, and, since you don't use any fat in the cooking process, it's a healthy way to cook.

Cooking chicken in a steamer over a pot of simmering water also gives succulent low-fat results. Poached and steamed chicken are both often finished off by pan-frying to give the meat an attractive bit of color.

SOUS-VIDE

Popular in restaurants for years but only recently in the home, cooking chicken sous-vide means vacuum-sealing the meat, then cooking it in a stove-top water bath at 50°F. Restaurants use a vacuum-sealer and a special bath but you can wrap the meat tightly in plastic wrap and aluminum foil, then cook it in a pot of water for an hour, maintaining an even temperature, and finish by pan-frying it in a hot pan. The method can be used on all cuts of meat to retain all the cooking juices.

about the recipes

"If you do what you've always done, you'll get what you've always got". That's something I heard years ago and it's as true in the kitchen as in any walk of life. Cooking is about developing your knowledge of food, understanding what makes the finest ingredients, learning how to use the right utensils, practicing your skills and—most of all—developing your own ideas and creating new dishes. And that's what I hope this book will help you to achieve.

I've put together a collection of recipes that put chicken center stage and explore its potential, using the whole range of different cuts and cooking methods, flavors and combinations of ingredients. You'll find the classics here, of course, but I've looked at every recipe with new eyes to give each one a modern twist, and show you imaginative and highly contemporary recipes that will offer you meals for every occasion, from street-smart snacks to dishes to wow your guests at your next dinner party.

But recipes don't work in isolation. To become favorites, they must respond to our lives. Dinner in our house most of the time involves putting something together quickly that tastes great and that everyone will enjoy—including the kids. At the weekends, I want to be a bit more relaxed, while when we have guests, I am cooking to impress. That's why I have divided the recipes into three lifetsyle-focused chapters: Weekday Meals, For the Weekend and Dinners & Celebrations.

WEEKDAY MEALS

Quick and easy is my weekday mantra—recipes focused on the days when life takes over and we seem to be constantly in a rush. With work, school, clubs and daily chores, we often have to fit mealtimes into the odd spaces that are left, and this chapter is packed with meals that fit that space neatly. If you are lucky, you may have an odd moment, either during the week or at the weekend, to prepare some dishes ahead of time to help things flow more smoothly—perhaps a stew or a couple of child-friendly snacks.

If you are looking for a light lunch, you'll find loads of choices, like Grilled Chicken, Fennel & Feta Salad (see page 33), Thai-Style Chicken Broth & Soba Noodles (see page 28) or Marcus's Ultimate Club Sandwich (see page 52). If it's something more substantial you are looking for, my Chicken, Basil Pesto & Zucchini Risotto (see page 61) won't disappoint—there's even a make-ahead, time-saving tip. There are lots of recipes to suit all the family, from my Spice-Rubbed, Roasted Half-chicken with Smoky-bacon French Fries (see page 74) to Chicken, Leek & Cream Linguine (see page 69).

FOR THE WEEKEND

The weekend may be more relaxed, but you still have plenty to do, so as well as some more creative dishes that demand a bit more time, there are Sunday roasts, things for the kids and some wonderful comfort foods. For a light meal, try my Chicken, Lemongrass & Thyme Scotch Eggs with Mustard Mayonnaise (see page 82). I have been refining this recipe for some years and now I feel I have got it exacty right, with the perfect crisp coating around the tasty ground meat with a zing of lemongrass to complement the thyme, and the runny yolk in the center. In my house, Chicken, Chorizo & Lima Bean Stew (see page 109) is a favorite, but we also love the pies, pastas, curries and quiches—and I'm sure you will, too.

DINNERS & CELEBRATIONS

Presentation and impact are crucial to impressing your friends with your culinary skills. You want things to look and taste great, but you want to enjoy the party, too, so the dishes in the final section fulfill both criteria—they are packed with plenty of the wow factor but are surprisingly quick to prepare. I'm a big fan of appetizers as if you spend the time to get the presentation and flavor right, you start your meal on the right note. Try Poached Chicken, Mango & Asparagus Verrine (see page 149) or Vietnamese Chicken & Pomegranate Seed Wraps with Sweet Chili Sauce (see page 161). Then balance the flavors in your appetizer with your main course. For a modern twist here, see how well flavors from different cuisines work together, as in Griddled Chicken Tikka on Lemongrass Sticks, which I serve with Belgian endive and tomatoes (see page 189).

FEATURE RECIPES

Each section also includes feature recipes that show off some of the classic partners to cook with chicken, marrying them together in unexpected ways. If you love the combination of chicken and mushrooms, Asian Chicken & Mushroom Ballotines (see page 172) will show them in a new light. Everyone loves chicken and french fries, but you'll never have tasted anything quite like my modern all-in-one version—Crisp Chicken & Potato Crust (see page 70).

Hopefully, these features will encourage you to start experimenting with your own dishes, substituting your favorite ingredients or adapting recipes to the seasons or the ingredients on hand. Cooking is about experimenting with flavors and finding out what works. I've created recipes to start you off, but don't ever be scared of trying to combine flavors and textures and trying something new. It's what makes you a great cook! So now you have been introduced to the stars of the show, nothing remains but to head for the kitchen and start cooking.

1

weekday
meals

Thai-style chicken broth & soba noodles

This recipe is a great example of a dish with stacks of flavor that is also really good for you. If you feel a cold coming on, you'll soon be back in the pink if you make yourself a steaming bowl of this powerful broth with its medicinal properties.

Bring the broth to a boil in a large pot over high heat. Thinly slice and mince the lower portion of the lemongrass stalk and leave the top of the stalk whole. Add the lemongrass to the broth along with the ginger, lime leaves, fish sauce, mirin, soy sauce, vinegar, chili, lime juice and bonito flakes, and stir well. Turn the heat down to low and simmer 5 minutes.

Meanwhile, bring a pot of water to a boil over high heat. Add the soba noodles, return to a boil and cook 5 minutes, then drain the noodles and put them in a bowl of ice-cold water to stop them cooking any further. Leave them in the water until needed.

Dust the chicken in the cornstarch, then add to the broth, stirring. Add the scallions and cilantro leaves, and simmer 4 to 5 minutes until the chicken is cooked through.

Drain the soba noodles and add them to the soup pot. Simmer until hot, about 2 minutes, then serve.

Serves 4
Preparation time: 20 minutes,
  plus making the stock
Cooking time: 15 minutes

3½ cups Chicken Broth (see page 197)
1 lemongrass stalk, cut in half
2-inch piece ginger root, peeled and
  thinly sliced into matchsticks
2 kaffir lime leaves
1 tablespoon Thai fish sauce
2 tablespoons mirin
2 tablespoons light soy sauce
1 tablespoon rice wine vinegar
1 red chili, seeded and thinly sliced into
  rings
juice of ½ lime
2 tablespoons dried bonito flakes
7 ounces dried soba noodles
2 skinless chicken breasts, thinly sliced
  into strips
2 teaspoons cornstarch
4 scallions, thinly sliced into rings
2 tablespoons cilantro leaves

Chicken Waterzooi

The Belgians are primarily known for their mussels and french fries, but this is a less well-known, traditional Belgian recipe for chicken. It's a rich, chunky soup that will keep you going throughout the day. You can also try it with fish instead of chicken.

Heat the oil and butter in a skillet over medium heat. Add the chicken and cook 1 to 2 minutes until just colored. Add the onions, garlic, carrots and leek and cook 3 to 4 minutes until lightly colored.

Add the broth and cream, turn the heat down to low and simmer 20 to 30 minutes until the vegetables are tender and the sauce has reduced slightly.

Put the egg yolk in a bowl and slowly whisk in a little of the soup until blended, then stir the mixture back into the soup. Stir in the chopped herbs and season with salt and pepper to taste.

Serve the hot soup with chunks of crusty bread.

Serves 4
Preparation time: 15 minutes,
  plus making the broth
Cooking time: 35 minutes

1 tablespoon olive oil
1 tablespoon unsalted butter
2 skinless chicken breasts, cubed
2 onions, finely chopped
2 garlic cloves, chopped
2 carrots, peeled and finely chopped
1 large leek, trimmed, cut in half and
  sliced
2 cups Chicken Broth (see page 197)
scant ½ cup heavy cream
1 large egg yolk
2 tablespoons chopped parsley leaves
1 tablespoon chopped chives
1 tablespoon chopped tarragon leaves
sea salt and freshly ground black pepper
crusty bread, to serve

Winter chicken Waldorf salad with crisp shallots

A winter version of the classic salad, this combines some excellent flavors from the coldest season. Make sure you choose some lovely juicy apples that are crisp and full of flavor, and top it off with some of my crisp fried shallots.

Heat the broiler to medium-high. Season the chicken with salt and pepper, put in a roasting pan and broil 6 to 7 minutes on each side, turning frequently, until the juices run clear when the thickest part of the chicken is pierced with the tip of a sharp knife.

Put all the salad ingredients in a bowl and toss together lightly. Chop the chicken into chunks and add to the salad ingredients.

Whisk together all the dressing ingredients in a separate bowl. Spoon a little of the dressing over the salad and gently toss together. Top with the crisp shallots to serve.

Serves 4
Preparation time: 15 minutes,
  plus making the mayonnaise
Cooking time: 15 minutes

3 skinless chicken breasts
3 red juicy apples, such as Pink Lady,
  cored and cut into small wedges
4 celery stalks, finely chopped
20 walnut halves, toasted
1 cup watercress
sea salt and freshly ground black pepper
1 recipe quantity Crisp Fried Shallots
  (see page 205), to serve

FOR THE WALDORF DRESSING
2 tablespoons walnut oil
1 teaspoon sherry vinegar
3 tablespoons Mayonnaise (see page 202)
1 teaspoon Dijon mustard
½ teaspoon lemon juice

Grilled chicken, fennel & feta salad

Simple salads make great lunches. Fresh, easy to put together, very healthy and with loads of flavors, you really can't go wrong. If you can grow a few herbs in your garden or on the window sill, you'll always have a fresh supply.

Rub a little oil all over the chicken pieces, then season with a little salt and pepper. Heat a ridged grill pan over high heat until smoking, or use a barbecue. Add the chicken to the grill pan and cook 3 to 4 minutes on each side until the juices run clear when the thickest part of the chicken is pierced with the tip of a sharp knife. Set aside.

Meanwhile, put all the remaining ingredients except the dressing in a bowl and toss together lightly. Slice the chicken and add it to the salad, then toss again. Drizzle with the dressing just before serving.

Serves 4
Preparation time: 5 minutes,
 plus making the dressing
Cooking time: 10 minutes

a little olive oil
4 skinlesss chicken breasts, sliced in half
 lengthwise
3 cups salad greens
1 cup shelled peas
2 small fennel bulbs, sliced into thin
 strips using a vegetable peeler
leaves from 4 dill sprigs, roughly chopped
leaves from 4 mint sprigs, roughly
 chopped
1$\frac{1}{3}$ cups crumbled feta cheese
2 tablespoons Bean House Salad Dressing
 (see page 203)
sea salt and freshly ground black pepper

Glazed orange & mustard chicken salad

There's a lovely contrast of tastes and textures in this dish, with the freshness of the orange contrasting with the rich mustard flavor. If you toss the chicken in the marinade before you go to work, it will take no time at all to put it together when you get home. For a more substantial dish, you could add parmentier potatoes (see page 214), sprinkling them over the salad just before serving.

Heat the oven to 400°F. Mix together all the marinade ingredients in a nonmetallic bowl. Season the chicken breasts with salt and pepper, then add to the bowl and toss the chicken in the marinade. Cover with plastic wrap and let marinate 30 minutes in the refrigerator.

Put the chicken in a roasting pan and roast 25 minutes, basting occasionally with a little of the marinade, until the juices run clear when the thickest part of the chicken is pierced with the tip of a sharp knife. If the chicken is getting too brown, cover it with aluminum foil until it has finished cooking.

Mix together the Swiss chard and baby spinach, season with salt and pepper to taste and drizzle a little of the dressing over them. Toss together well. Serve the chicken and salad with parmentier potatoes.

Serves 4
Preparation time: 10 minutes,
  plus 30 minutes marinating, and
  making the dressing
Cooking time: 25 minutes

4 skinless chicken breasts
12 Swiss chard leaves, finely chopped
3 cups baby spinach leaves
2 tablespoons Bean House Salad Dressing
  (see page 203)
sea salt and freshly ground black pepper
1 recipe quantity Parmentier Potatoes
  (see page 214) or new potatoes, to serve

**FOR THE ORANGE & MUSTARD
  MARINADE**
2 tablespoons orange marmalade
1 garlic clove, crushed and finely chopped
1 tablespoon Dijon mustard
1 tablespoon wholegrain mustard
grated zest and juice of ½ orange
1 tablespoon olive oil
1 tablespoon sherry vinegar

Quinoa, chicken & asparagus salad

I always remember my mom making a pie with this classic combination of chicken with asparagus. I have tried to give this great combo a new modern twist to highlight the subtle contrasts in flavor and texture, so I've kept the asparagus raw and peeled it thinly into strips, then used it in a salad with that fantastic, much-under-used grain, quinoa. This makes for a really healthy dish that I'm sure you will enjoy.

Bring a pot of water to a boil over high heat. Add the quinoa and return to a boil. Turn the heat down to low and simmer 10 to 15 minutes until tender. Drain through a fine strainer, then leave it to dry out for a couple of minutes.

Meanwhile, put the chicken in a bowl, pour in the oil and season with salt and pepper. Toss together to coat the chicken in the oil. Heat a ridged grill pan, then add the chicken and cook 5 minutes on each side until browned and the juices run clear when the thickest part of the chicken is pierced with the tip of a sharp knife. Remove from the broiler pan and let rest for a few minutes, then cut the chicken into thick slices.

Put the cooked quinoa in a bowl and add the chives and orange zest and juice. Season with salt and pepper to taste, then pile onto plates. Mix together the asparagus and carrot strips and pile on top of the quinoa. Top with the chicken, then scatter with the scallions and serve.

Serves 4
Preparation time: 15 minutes
Cooking time: 15 minutes

2/3 cup quinoa
4 skinless chicken breasts
2 tablespoons olive oil
3 tablespoons chopped chives
grated zest and juice of 1/2 orange
12 asparagus stems, cut into long, thin strips using a vegetable peeler
2 carrots, peeled and cut into long, thin strips using a vegetable peeler
8 scallions, thinly sliced into strips
sea salt and freshly ground black pepper

Thai-style chicken yuk sung

Yuk sung is a fresh and simple dish, but I always feel it could do with a bit more spice. So my version of the recipe uses chicken and Thai spices combined with sweet mango to give it a great flavor. It is ideal as a snack or appetizer or a sharing course for friends.

Mix together the mango, mint and lime leaf in a bowl, cover and chill in the refrigerator while you cook the chicken.

Heat half the oil in a large skillet over high heat until shimmering. Add the chicken and cook 2 minutes, stirring continuously. Remove the meat from the pan using a slotted spoon, put on a plate and set aside.

Heat the remaining oil and fry the garlic, chili and ginger for 1 minute. Add the lemongrass and fry 1 minute longer, then return the chicken to the pan along with the juices on the plate and mix everything together. Add the dark soy sauce, fish sauce, sugar and cilantro and mix thoroughly until hot.

Remove from the heat and spoon the mixture onto the lettuce leaves, piling it as high as you can. Top with the mango mixture and serve.

Serves 4
Preparation time: 10 minutes
Cooking time: 5 minutes

½ mango, peeled, pitted and finely chopped

4 mint leaves, roughly chopped

1 kaffir lime leaf, finely shredded

2 tablespoons peanut oil

2 skinless boneless chicken thighs, roughly chopped

2 garlic cloves, roughly chopped

½ red chili, including the seeds, roughly chopped

2-inch piece ginger root, peeled and roughly chopped

1 lemongrass stalk, peeled and finely chopped

½ tablespoon dark soy sauce

½ tablespoon Thai fish sauce

1 teaspoon palm sugar

2 tablespoons finely chopped cilantro leaves

8 small romaine lettuce leaves

Crisp sesame chicken strips with sweet & sour sauce

For this recipe, I use strips of chicken breast—known as inner fillets—cut from the underside of the breast. You can buy chicken fillets or cut one fillet from each chicken breast, then use the breasts for another recipe. You can make the sweet and sour sauce while the chicken is chilling.

Put the flour on a shallow plate and season with plenty of salt and pepper.

Mix together the breadcrumbs and the sesame seeds on a second shallow plate. Whisk together the eggs and milk in a third shallow plate to make an egg wash, then line the 3 plates up in a row. Lightly dust each chicken fillet in the flour, shaking off any excess. Dip in the egg wash, then coat with the breadcrumbs. Put them on a plate, cover lightly with plastic wrap and chill in the refrigerator for at least 10 minutes or until ready to use.

Heat the oil in a large, heavy skillet over medium heat, to 325°F, when a cube of bread browns in 60 seconds. Carefully put the fillets in the pan and cook 2 to 3 minutes on each side until cooked through and golden brown.

Drain the fillets on paper towels to remove any excess oil, then serve with the sweet and sour sauce and a herb salad.

Serves 4
Preparation time: 10 minutes, plus at least 10 minutes chilling
Cooking time: 10 minutes

heaped ⅓ cup all-purpose flour
1¾ cups panko breadcrumbs
¼ cup sesame seeds
2 eggs, beaten
3 tablespoons milk
10 skinless chicken inner fillets
⅔ cup peanut oil
sea salt and freshly ground black pepper
1 recipe quantity Sweet & Sour Sauce (see page 200), to serve
1 recipe quantity Herb Salad (see page 219), to serve

Chicken spring rolls with hoisin sauce

I don't always feel hungry after I've finished cooking, and at those times I just want a selection of little bites to eat. That's when these spring rolls really hit the spot, especially served with my homemade hoisin sauce. The kids love them, too, and they are much better for them than the store-bought versions. You can buy spring roll wrappers in most Asian food stores.

Heat the olive oil in a skillet over medium heat. Add the ground chicken and fry 4 to 5 minutes, stirring to break up the clumps, until browned and cooked through. Transfer to a bowl and let cool 3 to 4 minutes. Stir in the carrots, bean sprouts and soy sauce, and season with salt and pepper to taste. Whisk together the eggs, milk and a pinch of salt to make an egg wash.

Take 2 spring roll wrappers, and put one on top of the other. Put 2 tablespoons of the meat mixture in the center, brush a little of the egg wash around the edges, then fold over each end and roll up. Seal with a little egg wash on the join and set aside. Repeat until you have made 4 rolls.

Heat the peanut oil in a deep, heavy pot to 325°F, when a cube of bread browns in 60 seconds. Add the spring rolls, a few at a time if necessary, and cook 1 to 2 minutes until golden, then remove from the oil and drain on paper towels 1 minute. Serve hot with the hoisin sauce and a microleaf salad.

Serves 4
Preparation time: 15 minutes,
 plus making the hoisin sauce
Cooking time: 10 minutes

2 tablespoons olive oil
2¼ cups ground chicken
2 carrots, peeled and cut into matchsticks
2 cups bean sprouts
2 tablespoons light soy sauce
2 eggs
2 teaspoons milk
2 x 14-ounce packages spring roll
 wrappers
peanut oil, for deep-frying
sea salt and freshly ground black pepper
1 recipe quantity Hoisin Sauce (see page
 200), to serve
1 recipe quantity Microleaf & Carrot Salad
 (see page 219), to serve

Chicken fajitas & homemade smoked paprika wraps

Fajitas have always been my choice for an informal meal with friends and before I started cooking, we'd make them right from a fajita kit. But once I started to cook I wanted to make my perfect feast even better by cooking everything from scratch—and it's so worth it. Plus fajitas are so quick to make, they are great for midweek meals for your family or when you invite a few friends round for supper. Your friends are sure to be impressed—and they'll enjoy it all the more if you stock up on a few bottles of Mexican beer to wash it down.

Put the chicken in a bowl, drizzle with the oil and season with salt and pepper.

Heat a ridged grill pan over high heat until it just starts to smoke, then add the chicken, in batches if necessary, and cook 1 to 2 minutes on each side until it has charred markings. Repeat with the peppers.

Serve the chicken and peppers with the wraps, sour cream, salsa and guacamole so your guests can wrap and enjoy their own fajitas.

Serves 4
Preparation time: 10 minutes, plus making the wraps, salsa and guacamole
Cooking time: 20 minutes

4 skinless chicken breasts, cut into 8 even-size strips
2 tablespoons olive oil
1 red bell pepper, seeded and cut into strips
1 green bell pepper, seeded and cut into strips
sea salt and freshly ground black pepper

TO SERVE
1 recipe quantity Smoked Paprika Wraps (see page 209)
¼ cup sour cream
1 recipe quantity Tomato Salsa (see page 201)
1 recipe quantity Guacamole (see page 201)

Mango & cilantro coronation-chicken pita pockets

Coronation chicken is a great British classic, with its balance of spicy and sweet Anglo-Indian flavors. I love making my own curry powder so I can make it as spicy or aromatic as I want. Once the chicken mixture is made, it will keep in the refrigerator for 4 to 5 days. Those who like to take a nutritious lunch to work need look no further as these make the perfect portable lunch.

Put all the spices in a small pan and set over medium heat about 4 minutes until they just start to warm through and release a spicy aroma. Tip into a small spice grinder or mortar and pestle and grind until you have a fine powder.

Add a teaspoonful of the curry powder to the mayonnaise and season with salt and pepper to taste. Add more curry powder to the mayonnaise, if you like. Fold in the chicken.

Toast the pita breads on both sides, then cut each one across widthways to make 2 pita pockets. Fill them with the coronation chicken mixture, then top with the mango and cilantro. Eat on their own as a quick snack or with homemade sweet potato crisps.

Serves 4
Preparation time: 10 minutes,
  plus making the mayonnaise
Cooking time: 5 minutes

3 to 4 tablespoons Mayonnaise
  (see page 202)
1 pound poached skinless chicken breasts
  (see page 23), shredded or cut into
  chunks
4 wholewheat or white pita breads
1 ripe mango, peeled, pitted and cubed
1 cup cilantro leaves, chopped
sea salt and freshly ground black pepper
1 recipe quantity Sweet Potato Crisps
  (see page 215), to serve

FOR THE CURRY POWDER
1/2 teaspoon ground cardamom
1/2 star anise
1 tablespoon coriander seeds
1 tablespoon turmeric
1/2 tablespoon fenugreek seeds
1 tablespoon ground cumin
2 teaspoons mustard seeds
1/2 teaspoon fennel seeds
1 teaspoon dried red pepper flakes
1 tablespoon olive oil

Chicken, tomato & arugula pesto arancini

A delicious risotto-style mixture, coated in breadcrumbs and fried until golden, arancini are a Sicilian specialty that uses up leftover risotto. Hot or cold, these fried rice balls make the perfect snack food for a busy day—filling, fresh and full of flavor.

Put the risotto in a bowl and mix in the chicken, tomatoes and a spoonful of pesto. Season with salt and pepper to taste. Shape the rice mixture into about 8 small balls.

Whisk together the eggs and milk in a shallow bowl to make an egg wash. Mix the breadcrumbs and parmesan in another shallow bowl. One at a time, dip the arancini in the egg wash, coating all sides, then shake off any excess and roll each ball in the breadcrumb mixture until coated.

Heat the oil in a deep, heavy pot to 325°F, when a cube of day-old bread will brown in 60 seconds. Gently lower the arancini, one at a time, into the hot oil and cook about 3 minutes until golden.

Drain on paper towels, then serve with extra pesto for dipping. They make delicious canapés for cocktail parties, are lovely as an appetizer, or you can serve them with a mixed salad for a light lunch or dinner.

Serves 4
Preparation time: 15 minutes, plus
  30 minutes cooling, and making the
  slow-roasted tomatoes and pesto
Cooking time: 25 minutes

2 cups leftover risotto rice or risotto base
  (see page 61), chilled
1 to 2 poached or roasted chicken breasts
  (see page 23), skinned, shredded and
  finely chopped
1/3 cup Slow-Roasted Tomatoes (see page
  218), drained and finely chopped
1 to 2 tablespoons Fresh Arugula Pesto
  (see page 201), plus extra to serve
2 eggs, beaten
a small splash of milk
2 1/2 cups panko breadcrumbs
2/3 cup shredded parmesan cheese
peanut oil, for deep-frying
sea salt and freshly ground black pepper

Chicken falafel with cucumber raita

The simplest dishes often give the best results and this fits the bill. I've made it from scratch for this recipe but it is also a good way to use leftover cooked chicken from your Sunday roast—just leave out the first step and start by blitzing your falafel ingredients.

Bring the broth to a boil in a pot over medium heat. Add the chicken, turn the heat down to low and simmer 15 to 20 minutes until the juices run clear when the thickest part of the chicken is pierced with the tip of a sharp knife. Drain, then shred the chicken with two forks while it is still hot.

Put all the falafel ingredients except the chicken into a blender and blitz until well blended. Tip into a bowl, add the chicken, season with salt and pepper and mix together. Use your hands to shape into about 24 small balls, then dust with flour.

Heat the oil in a deep, heavy pot to 325°F, when a cube of bread browns in 60 seconds. Fry the falafels about 4 minutes until golden brown. Remove using a slotted spoon and drain on paper towels.

Meanwhile, put the yogurt in a bowl, stir in the mint and cucumber and season with salt and pepper to taste.

Serve the chicken falafels and yogurt with a tomato, feta, onion and mint salad.

Serves: 4
Preparation time: 15 minutes, plus overnight soaking, and making the broth
Cooking time: 25 minutes

1¼ cups Chicken Broth (see page 197)
3 skinless chicken breasts, quartered
2⅓ cups dried chickpeas, soaked overnight, then drained
1 onion, finely chopped
2 garlic cloves
1 tablespoon gram (chickpea) flour
1 tablespoon ground cumin
2 tablespoons chopped cilantro leaves
½ the seeds from 1 black cardamom pod
¼ teaspoon cayenne pepper
½ teaspoon turmeric
2 tablespoons tahini paste
10 ounces cooked sweet potato
1 egg yolk
a little all-purpose flour, for dusting
peanut oil, for deep-frying
sea salt and freshly ground black pepper
tomato, feta, red onion and mint salad, to serve

FOR THE CUCUMBER RAITA
¾ cup plain yogurt
2 tablespoons chopped mint leaves
heaped ⅓ cup peeled, seeded and grated English cucumber

Smoky bacon chicken wings

If you have been browsing through my recipes, you may have already noticed that pancetta, a type of Italian bacon, is one of my favorite ingredients—the slow curing process gives it such a fantastic flavor that goes so well with chicken, which absorbs the strong flavors and somehow seems to improve on them. There are so many recipes for chicken wrapped in bacon that I wanted to add a new twist, so I've cooked the pancetta in the oven until crisp, then mixed it with sugar and spice to make a bacon rub to add to the chicken wings and transform them into a tasty, spicy snack.

Heat the oven to 400°F. Put the strips of pancetta on a baking sheet and bake 15 minutes until dark and crisp. Remove from the oven and let cool.

Put into a spice grinder or blender and blitz to a powder, then add the sugar, smoked paprika and cayenne and blitz quickly again.

Put the chicken wings in a bowl and rub all the smoky bacon mixture into the wings. Spread them out on a baking sheet, making sure there is plenty of the bacon mixture on top of the wings so it melts as they cook. Roast 20 minutes until the chicken wings are colored and cooked through. Serve warm on their own as a smoky and spicy snack.

Serves 4
Preparation time: 10 minutes
Cooking time: 35 minutes

8 strips of pancetta
2 teaspoons dark brown sugar
2 teaspoons smoked paprika
1/2 teaspoon cayenne pepper
16 chicken wings

Southern fried chicken & chili corn

Delicious, inexpensive and easy to make, I think just about everyone must have tried this at one time or another but perhaps not made it for themselves. There's no reason to be hesitant as you can follow this simple recipe to make the perfect crisp chicken with a side of chili corn.

Put the chicken pieces in a bowl. Mix together the buttermilk and Tabasco, pour it over the chicken and turn to mix together. Cover with plastic wrap and let marinate in the refrigerator for 8 hours or overnight.

Drain the chicken pieces, reserving the buttermilk marinade in a shallow bowl. Heat the oven to 350°F. Heat 1½ inches of oil in a heavy pot over medium heat to 350°F, when a cube of bread browns in 60 seconds.

While the oil is heating, mix the flour with the spices and herbs in a shallow bowl. Dip the first chicken piece in the buttermilk, shake off any excess, then coat it all over in the flour. Lower into the hot oil and fry 2 to 3 minutes until golden in color. As it is cooking, continue with the next piece, adding them to the pot in a clockwise direction so you know which will be finished first. As each piece is cooked, transfer to a baking sheet using a slotted spoon. When they are all cooked, place in the oven and bake 5 to 10 minutes, or until the coating is crisp and golden brown and the juices run clear when the thickest part of the chicken is pierced with the tip of a sharp knife.

Meanwhile, bring a large pot of water to a boil over high heat. Add the corn and return to a boil. Cook 4–5 minutes, then drain.

Put the butter and chili in a bowl, season well with salt and pepper and mix together. Smear the cobs with the chili butter and serve with the chicken pieces.

Serves 4
Preparation time: 10 minutes, plus overnight marinating
Cooking time: 20 minutes

12 chicken drumsticks or thighs, skin on
2 cups buttermilk
1 teaspoon Tabasco
olive oil, for deep-frying
1 cup self-rising flour
2 tablespoons smoked paprika
1 tablespoon sea salt
1 tablespoon freshly ground black pepper
1 teaspoon cayenne pepper
1 teaspoon chili powder
2 teaspoons chopped thyme leaves
4 ears of corn, cut into chunks
3½ tablespoons unsalted butter
1 red chili, seeded and finely chopped

Marcus's ultimate club sandwich

Sometimes I crave nothing more than a good sandwich and, of course, the club sandwich is the ultimate. For the best results, use homemade toasted bread or a freshly baked artisan bread from a local bakery. Chicken and smoked bacon are a great combination and with slow-roasted tomatoes and the avocado salsa, it works just perfectly.

Heat the oven to 425°F. Put the bacon on a baking sheet and bake 15 to 20 minutes until just crisp. Set aside until needed. Turn the oven to 400°F.

Season the chicken with a little salt. Heat the oil in a large, stovetop and ovenproof dish over medium-high heat. Add the chicken and cook 2 to 3 minutes on each side until just browned. Transfer the dish to the oven and cook 15 to 20 minutes until the juices run clear when the thickest part of the chicken is pierced with the tip of a sharp knife. (Omit this step if you are using cooked chicken.)

To make the avocado salsa, cut the avocado in half, discard the pit and scoop out all the flesh into a bowl. Squeeze in the lime juice, then crush the avocado with the back of a fork to make a paste. Stir in the cilantro and season with salt and pepper to taste.

Toast the bread on both sides, then butter the slices on one side. Spread a layer of mayonnaise on the buttered side of 4 slices of bread, then put 2 bacon strips on top, then the red onion and finally the slow-roasted tomatoes on top. Put another slice of buttered bread on top of each pile, then spread the tops with half the avocado mixture. Slice the chicken and put on the top, then add the arugula, season with a little salt and pepper, then top with the remaining slices of bread, buttered-side down.

Gently press the sandwiches to pack them down, then cut them in half and pierce each half with a skewer to hold them together. Serve with the remaining avocado salsa and with homemade sweet potato crisps, if you like.

Serves 4
Preparation time: 15 minutes, plus making the mayonnaise and slow-roasted tomatoes
Cooking time: 40 minutes

8 strips smoked Canadian bacon
4 skinless chicken breasts, or use leftover cooked chicken
1 tablespoon olive oil
12 slices of homemade or artisan bread
3½ tablespoons salted butter, at room temperature
¼ cup Mayonnaise (see page 202)
9 ounces Slow-Roasted Tomatoes (see page 218)
1 small red onion, thinly sliced
2 cups arugula leaves
sea salt and freshly ground black pepper
1 recipe quantity Sweet Potato Crisps (see page 215), to serve (optional)

FOR THE AVOCADO SALSA
1 ripe avocado
½ lime
1 teaspoon chopped cilantro leaves

Chicken & slow-roasted tomato burgers with pesto mayonnaise

I do love a good burger. My tip for success is to build on the flavor of the ground chicken, starting with the onion and garlic, then adding herbs and sauces. My special ingredient in this burger is the slow-roasted tomatoes, which lift the flavors and give a lovely, fresh kick. Combine it with the fresh basil pesto mayonnaise and you have something really special.

Heat the oven to 400°F. Put the ground chicken in a bowl and add the tomatoes, onion, garlic, thyme, truffle oil, if using, breadcrumbs and Worcestershire sauce and Tabasco, and mix together well until combined. Shape into 4 burgers, then cover and chill 20 minutes in the refrigerator to firm up while you start to cook the sweet potato wedges.

Meanwhile, mix together the pesto and mayonnaise, cover and chill in the refrigerator until ready to use.

Heat the olive oil in a ridged grill pan or heavy skillet over medium-high heat. Add the burgers and cook 3 to 4 minutes on each side until browned, turning the heat down to low if they start to brown too quickly. Transfer to the oven and cook 5 to 10 minutes with the sweet potatoes until cooked through and browned.

Remove the burgers from the oven, cover and let rest in a warm place while you toast the bread rolls. Put some arugula leaves on the bottom half of each bun, top with a spoonful of the pesto mayonnaise, then the burger, another spoonful of pesto mayonnaise, then the remaining bun. Serve with the sweet potato wedges.

Serves 4
Preparation time: 20 minutes, plus
  20 minutes chilling, and making the
  slow-roasted tomatoes, pesto and
  mayonnaise
Cooking time: 30 minutes

1¼ pounds ground chicken
10 ounces Slow-Roasted Tomatoes (see
  page 218) or sun-dried tomatoes (not in
  oil), finely chopped
1 onion, chopped
2 garlic bulbs, crushed and chopped
leaves from 2 thyme sprigs, chopped
1 recipe quantity Sweet Potato Wedges
  (see page 215), to serve
2 teaspoons truffle oil (optional)
2 tablespoons breadcrumbs
2 teaspoons Worcestershire sauce
½ teaspoon Tabasco
1 tablespoon olive oil
4 bread rolls, sliced in half
1 handful of arugula leaves
sea salt and freshly ground black pepper

FOR THE PESTO MAYONNAISE
2 tablespoons Fresh Basil Pesto
  (see page 201)
¼ cup Mayonnaise (see page 202)

Chicken schnitzel with sorrel mayonnaise

A schnitzel is a boneless piece of meat that has been flattened out, then egg washed, bread-crumbed and fried. The dish originated in Austria and Germany, and traditionally would have used veal. I really enjoy a bit of fried chicken and the beauty of this recipe is it is super-quick to cook and the chicken stays really tender. Plus you can serve it with any kind of potatoes and vegetables. The delicious sorrel mayonnaise gives it a contemporary twist.

Place each chicken breast between two layers of plastic wrap and use a rolling pin to bash them until they are about ⅝ inch thick.

Put the flour on a shallow plate and season with plenty of salt and pepper. Mix together the breadcrumbs, fennel seeds and rosemary on a second shallow plate. Whisk together the eggs and milk in a third shallow plate, then line the 3 plates up in a row. Lightly dust each chicken breast in the flour, shaking off any excess. Dip them in the egg, then coat with the breadcrumbs. Put them on a plate, cover lightly with plastic wrap and chill 10 minutes in the refrigerator, or until needed.

Meanwhile, heat the oil in a large skillet over medium-high heat. If your pan will not hold all the schnitzels comfortably, cook them in batches. Gently put the schnitzels in the pan and cook 2 to 3 minutes on each side until cooked through and golden brown.

Mix the sorrel and lemon juice into the mayonnaise, then season with salt and pepper to taste. Serve the chicken and sorrel mayonnaise with sweet potato wedges and some green beans.

Serves 4
Preparation time: 30 minutes, plus 10 minutes chilling, and making the mayonnaise
Cooking time: 15 minutes

4 skinless chicken breasts
⅓ cup all-purpose flour
1½ cups panko breadcrumbs
1 teaspoon fennel seeds
1 teaspoon chopped rosemary leaves
2 eggs, beaten
⅓ cup milk
⅓ cup olive oil
sea salt and freshly ground black pepper
1 recipe quantity Sweet Potato Wedges (see page 215), to serve
steamed green beans, to serve

FOR THE SORREL MAYONNAISE
¼ cup chopped sorrel leaves or spinach leaves
juice of 1 lemon
1 recipe quantity Mayonnaise (see page 202)

Chicken & broccoli soufflé omelet

I'm a big fan of omelets as they are so quick to make, plus they are great for using up all sorts of cooked or leftover ingredients—in this case, chicken and broccoli—making them perfect for a quick and easy midweek meal. (By the way, try steaming broccoli when you cook it to keep the lovely green color.) Most of all, eggs are full of protein and really good for you. For this recipe, I've given it that modern tweak by using extra egg whites. This really lifts the omelet and makes it a lot lighter and fluffier.

Heat the oven to 350°F and cut out a circle of parchment paper that will fit the inside of a large, ovenproof skillet.

Whisk the eggs in a large bowl until light, then season with salt and pepper and add the chives. In a separate bowl, beat the eggs whites, using an electric beater (unless you're feeling energetic!), until soft peaks form. Carefully fold the egg whites into the beaten egg, using a large metal spoon, then stir in the chicken and broccoli.

Heat the butter and oil in a large ovenproof skillet over medium-high heat. When the pan is hot and the butter is foaming, add the egg mixture and cook 2 to 3 minutes until the bottom is beginning to set, then sprinkle with the cheese, cover with the prepared parchment paper and transfer the pan to the oven for 3 to 4 minutes until the soufflé omelet has risen and is just set in the center. Turn out onto a plate or serve right from the pan.

Serves 4
Preparation time: 10 minutes,
  plus making the confit
Cooking time: 7 minutes

8 eggs
2 tablespoons chopped chives
4 egg whites
10½ ounces Confit Chicken
  (see page 122), cubed
3 cups broccoli, cut into tiny florets and
  steamed
2 tablespoons unsalted butter
2 tablespoons olive oil
⅔ cup shredded strongly flavored hard
  cheese, such as a sharp cheddar
sea salt and freshly ground black pepper

Blackened chicken with Mediterranean vegetable couscous

Couscous makes the perfect partner for this spice-blackened chicken. If you pop the chicken in the refrigerator to marinate before you go to work, it will be ready to cook as soon as you get home, and even more full of flavor from a longer time marinating. Toasting the couscous beforehand also adds to the nutty flavor.

Mix together all the marinade ingredients in a nonmetallic bowl, add the chicken and turn it so it is coated in the marinade. Cover and let marinate at least 20 minutes in the refrigerator.

Heat the oven to 400°F. While the oven is heating up, soak the couscous.

Remove the chicken from the marinade and put it into a roasting pan. Roast 15 to 20 minutes until blackened on the outside and the juices run clear when the thickest part of the chicken is pierced with the tip of a sharp knife.

Let the chicken rest 2 minutes, then slice and serve on top of the couscous.

Serves 4
Preparation time: 25 minutes, plus at least 20 minutes marinating, and making the broth
Cooking time: 20 minutes

4 skinless chicken breasts, lightly scored
1¾ cups Vegetable Broth (see page 197)
1 recipe quantity Mediterranean Vegetable Couscous (see page 211)
sea salt and freshly ground black pepper

FOR THE BLACKENED CHICKEN MARINADE
1 teaspoon ground cumin
1 teaspoon ground fennel seeds
1 teaspoon smoked paprika
¼ teaspoon ground ginger
1 tablespoon dark brown sugar
2 tablespoons light soy sauce
1 teaspoon balsamic vinegar
1 teaspoon chopped thyme leaves
1 tablespoon tomato paste
¼ teaspoon cayenne pepper

Chicken, basil pesto & zucchini risotto

Once you master the basics of risotto, the options are endless. To make it easier on busy weekdays, you can make the base ahead of time, then finish it off just before serving. If you like, you could top it with some of my crisp fried shallots.

Heat the oil and butter in a large skillet over medium heat. Add the onion and garlic and fry 5 minutes, stirring occasionally, until softened. Stir in the rice to coat it in the onion mixture. Pour in the wine and stir until it is absorbed by the rice.

Add a small ladleful of the hot broth and stir until the broth is absorbed by the rice before adding the next ladleful. Add the zucchini, then continue adding ladlefuls of the broth, stirring so the rice cooks evenly, until you have used half of the broth. This should take about 10 minutes. This is the risotto base and it can be left at this stage, if more convenient, and the dish finished later. If you want to do this, transfer the rice to a container that has a lid and let cool completely, uncovered. When cool, cover and chill in the refrigerator for up to 2 days.

To cook the chicken, heat the oven to 350°F. Heat the oil in an ovenproof skillet over medium-high heat. Season the chicken with salt and pepper, add to the pan and fry 3 minutes on each side to color, then transfer the pan to the oven and cook 15 minutes until the juices run clear when the thickest part of the chicken is pierced with the tip of a sharp knife. Remove from the oven, cover and let rest 2 to 3 minutes, then slice into strips.

To finish the risotto, reheat the reserved broth. Return the risotto base to the large pan over medium-low heat. Continue to add the broth a ladleful at a time about 10 minutes, stirring continuously, until the broth is absorbed and the rice is tender but still retains some bite.

Stir the pesto and chicken into the rice, then stir in the cream, parmesan and lemon juice, and season with salt and pepper. Sprinkle with the chives and some extra parmesan, and serve with salad and crisp shallots, if you like.

Serves 4
Preparation time: 20 minutes,
  plus making the broth and pesto
Cooking time: 35 minutes

FOR THE RISOTTO BASE
1 tablespoon olive oil
⅓ cup unsalted butter
1 large onion, finely chopped
2 garlic cloves, finely chopped
1⅓ cups risotto rice, such as arborio
¾ cup dry white wine
3¼ cups hot Vegetable Broth
  (see page 197)
1 zucchini, finely chopped

FOR THE RISOTTO
2 tablespoons olive oil
4 skinless chicken breasts
3 to 4 tablespoons Fresh Basil Pesto
  (see page 201)
½ cup heavy cream
½ cup shredded parmesan cheese,
  plus extra for serving
juice and zest of ½ lemon
1 tablespoon chives
sea salt and freshly ground black pepper

TO SERVE
Herb Salad (see page 219) or a Green
  Salad (see page 219)
1 recipe quantity Crisp Fried Shallots
  (see page 205) (optional)

Chicken, chorizo & tiger shrimp paella

Sometimes you just want to cook a simple one-pot dish that will give you lots of flavor and feed lots of people. For those moments, this is the perfect recipe, and I guarantee the whole family will love it, even the kids. It's certainly a favorite with my daughters.

Heat the oil and butter in a large, nonstick skillet over medium heat. Add the onion and garlic and cook 3 minutes until softened. Add the chorizo and cook 1 minute, then add the red pepper, turmeric and smoked paprika, then the rice, and cook 2 minutes, stirring.

Add the chicken and half the broth. Bring to a boil over medium-high heat, then turn the heat down to low and simmer about 10 to 12 minutes, stirring occasionally, until most of the liquid is absorbed.

Add the shrimp, peas and the remaining broth, bring to a boil, then turn the heat down to low and simmer gently 8 to 10 minutes longer until almost all the liquid is absorbed and the chicken and shrimp are cooked. Season with salt and pepper to taste, then add the parsley.

Serve the paella on its own for a simple, impressive and delicious supper.

Serves 4
Preparation time: 15 minutes,
  plus making the broth
Cooking time: 30 minutes

¼ cup olive oil
2 tablespoons unsalted butter
1 large onion, finely chopped
2 garlic cloves, crushed
5½ ounces chorizo, cut into chunks
1 large red bell pepper, seeded and sliced
1 teaspoon turmeric
1 tablespoon smoked paprika
1 heaped cup paella or risotto rice,
  such as arborio
14 ounces chicken fillet strips, cut into
  chunks
2½ cups Chicken Broth (see page 197)
7 ounces raw tiger shrimp, unpeeled
⅔ cup fresh shelled or frozen peas
2 tablespoons chopped parsley leaves
sea salt and freshly ground black pepper

Chicken, bok choy & toasted peanut stir-fry

Stir-frys are another great way to rustle up a quick, healthy and interesting meal when you are pushed for time. Make sure your pan is hot when you add the ingredients and keep them moving around the pan all the time so they cook evenly and do not burn.

Dust the chicken strips lightly in the cornstarch. Heat a wok or skillet over high heat. Add the sesame oil and fish sauce, then add the chicken strips and fry 1 minute, stirring continuously.

Add the garlic, bok choy, peanuts and bean sprouts, and toss together. Add the vinegar, soy sauce and broth, stir together well and bring to a boil. Cook 2 minutes longer, still stirring, until the chicken is cooked through and the sauce has reduced and thickened. Season with salt and pepper to taste. Serve right away and enjoy.

Serves 4
Preparation time: 10 minutes,
  plus making the broth
Cooking time: 10 minutes

4 skinless chicken breasts, cut into strips
1 tablespoon cornstarch
1 tablespoon sesame oil
1 teaspoon Thai fish sauce
1 garlic clove, chopped
4 bok choy, cut in half
$\frac{1}{2}$ cup peanuts
$1\frac{1}{2}$ cups bean sprouts
1 tablespoon raspberry vinegar
1 tablespoon light soy sauce
scant $\frac{2}{3}$ cup Chicken Broth (see page 197)
sea salt and freshly ground black pepper

Chicken with crisp noodles

A quick and easy stir-fry that makes a great lunch or supper dish, this is perfect for the busy lives we all lead—and it's healthy too. I'm also convinced that you'll love my simple, new twist of combining the chicken with crisp, instead of soft, noodles.

Bring a pot of water to a boil over high heat. Add the egg noodles and cook 3 to 4 minutes until tender. Drain well, then divide the noodles into four piles.

Heat at least 2 inches of the peanut oil in a deep, heavy pot to 350°F, when a cube of bread browns in 50 seconds. Using a large slotted spoon, lower the first pile of noodles into the oil and fry about 1 minute until golden, then lift them back out and drain on paper towels. Repeat with the remaining noodles. Keep them warm until needed.

Meanwhile, heat the sesame oil in a large skillet over medium heat. Add the garlic and chicken and fry 2 minutes, stirring. Add the peppers and carrots and fry 2 to 3 minutes longer until the peppers are just soft. Add the mirin, vinegar and soy sauce, and stir well, then add the cabbage. Turn the heat up to high and stir-fry a few minutes until all the ingredients are well blended and the chicken is cooked through.

Put the crisp noodle nests on plates, spoon the chicken into the center with a little sauce—and it's time to eat.

Serves 4
Preparation time: 15 minutes
Cooking time: 10 minutes

10 ounces egg noodles
peanut oil, for deep-frying
1 tablespoon sesame oil
2 garlic cloves, finely chopped
4 skinless chicken breasts, cut into thin
　strips
½ red bell pepper, seeded and finely
　chopped
½ green bell pepper, seeded and finely
　chopped
2 carrots, peeled and cut into fine
　matchsticks
1 teaspoon mirin
1 teaspoon rice wine vinegar
¼ cup light soy sauce
1 spring cabbage or other dark green leafy
　cabbage, thinly sliced

Chicken macaroni & cheese with crisp pancetta

I love the change of texture and added interest that you get by adding chicken to macaroni and cheese, so that's what I've done with this recipe. Plus I've spiced it up with a little mustard and included some crisp pancetta for a more rounded flavor. This is the kind of classic recipe that doesn't need to be radically modernized because it is so good, just tweaked a little.

Heat the oven to 350°F. Line a baking sheet with parchment paper and lay the strips of pancetta on top, then cover with another sheet of parchment paper and top with a second baking sheet to press them as they cook. Bake 10 to 12 minutes until flat and crisp, then let cool.

Meanwhile, heat the oil in a skillet over medium-high heat. Season the chicken with salt and pepper, add it to the pan and fry 2 minutes on each side until lightly colored. Very carefully add scant ½ cup water—it will sizzle and spit—turn the heat down to low, partially cover and cook about 10 minutes until the juices run clear when the thickest part of the chicken is pierced with the tip of a sharp knife. Remove from the pan and cut into small pieces.

While the chicken is cooking, bring a large pot of lightly salted water to a boil, add the macaroni and return to a boil. Simmer 10 to 12 minutes until just tender. Drain well, then return it to the hot pot and drizzle a little oil over the pasta to stop it sticking together.

Melt the butter in a pot over medium-high heat, then add the onion and garlic and cook 2 minutes until softened. Add the flour and cook 1 minute longer, stirring, then gradually add the milk, stirring continuously as the sauce starts to thicken. Stir in the mascarpone and the mustards, then three quarters of the cheddar cheese and keep stirring until melted. Add the chicken and season with salt and pepper to taste.

Stir the cheese sauce into the macaroni and spoon it into an ovenproof dish. Sprinkle with the remaining cheddar cheese and bake 15 minutes until the cheese is melted and golden. Top with the pancetta and serve with a salad.

Serves 4
Preparation time: 20 minutes
Cooking time: 40 minutes

8 slices of pancetta
1 tablespoon olive oil, plus extra for drizzling
2 skinless chicken breasts
9 ounces macaroni
1 teaspoon salt
3 tablespoons unsalted butter
1 onion, finely chopped
1 garlic clove, finely chopped
⅓ cup all-purpose flour
2 cups milk
1 tablespoon mascarpone cheese
1 teaspoon Dijon mustard
½ teaspoon English or strong mustard
1⅔ cups shredded sharp cheddar cheese
freshly ground black pepper
1 recipe quantity Microleaf & Carrot Salad (see page 219), to serve

Chicken, leek & cream linguine

Heat the oven to 400°F. Season the chicken with salt and pepper. Heat half the oil in a heavy skillet over medium-high heat and fry the chicken 2 to 3 minutes on each side until browned, then transfer to a roasting pan. Roast 10 to 12 minutes, or until the juices run clear when the thickest part of the chicken is pierced with the tip of a sharp knife. Let the cooked chicken rest in a warm place.

Meanwhile, bring a pot of water to a boil over high heat. Add the leeks and blanch for 30 seconds, then drain, refresh in ice-cold water, drain again and set aside.

Melt the butter and the remaining oil in a skillet over medium-low heat. Add the shallots, garlic, lemon zest and a little salt, and fry 3 minutes until softened but not brown. Turn the heat up to high, add the wine and boil 4 to 5 minutes until almost all the wine has evaporated. Add the broth and boil to reduce again by two thirds. Reduce the heat to low, add the cream and simmer a few minutes until the sauce has slightly thickened and coats the back of a spoon.

While the sauce is cooking, bring another pot of salted water to a boil over high heat. Add the linguine, return to a boil and cook about 5 minutes, or as directed on the package. Drain and keep warm.

Strain the sauce through a fine mesh strainer into a clean pot, pushing the shallots with the back of a spoon to make sure all the flavor is squeezed out. Discard the shallots. Bring the cream sauce back to a simmer over medium heat and stir in the mustard and lemon juice. Season with salt and pepper to taste.

Spoon the pasta into serving bowls and pour the sauce over it. Scatter the leeks and chives on top, then slice the chicken and arrange it on top of the creamy pasta. Serve with a fresh, green salad.

Serves 4
Preparation time: 15 minutes, plus making the broth
Cooking time: 20 minutes

4 chicken breasts, skin on
2 tablespoons olive oil
5 baby leeks, trimmed and sliced on the diagonal
2 tablespoons unsalted butter
4 shallots, sliced
2 garlic cloves, skin left on, crushed
2 strips of lemon zest
¾ cup dry white wine
¾ cup Chicken Broth (see page 197)
¾ cup heavy cream
10 ounces linguine
1 tablespoon wholegrain mustard
a small squeeze of lemon juice
1 tablespoon very finely chopped chives
sea salt and freshly ground black pepper
1 recipe quantity Green Salad (see page 219), to serve

Crisp chicken & potato crust

This unusul twist on the classic combination of chicken and french fries is a real crowd pleaser, offering a modern interpretation of this great pairing—succulent meat and crunchy, golden potatoes. It makes for a filling yet impressive dish for any occasion. Cutting the chicken into strips makes it super child-friendly, but you can cook the chicken breasts whole if you prefer, then slice them on the diagonal to serve, giving the dish a slightly more grown-up look. It also goes really well with buttered carrots or kale.

Heat the oven to 315°F. Season the chicken breasts with salt and pepper. Put the grated potatoes on a shallow plate and press with paper towels to soak up any excess moisture. Whisk the eggs in a second shallow plate. Put the flour on a third shallow plate and season with salt and pepper. Toss the potatoes in the flour, shaking off any excess. Press the chicken strips into the potato mixture, shaping it around and pressing gently to seal the chicken within the grated potato casing.

Heat the oil and butter in a skillet over medium-high heat. Add the potato-wrapped chicken a few pieces at a time and cook about 12 minutes until golden brown on all sides and the juices run clear when the thickest part of the chicken is pierced with the tip of a sharp knife. Keep the cooked chicken warm in the oven while you cook the rest.

Serve the chicken with hot mushy peas.

Serves 4
Preparation time: 25 minutes
Cooking time: 30 minutes

4 skinless chicken breasts, cut into thick strips
6 to 8 large baking potatoes, peeled and grated but not rinsed
1 egg, beaten
2 tablespoons all-purpose flour
2 to 3 tablespoons olive oil
2 tablespoons unsalted butter
sea salt and freshly ground black pepper
British canned mushy peas or frozen peas, to serve

Chive chicken with creamed cabbage

You can make this with statler breasts or regular chicken breasts—either way it is really quick to make for a tasty midweek meal. Try it with smoked bacon for a change. I like to serve it with creamy mashed potatoes but it would go well with boiled potatoes or rice, too.

Heat the oven to 375°F and season the chicken with salt and pepper. Heat half the oil in a large, heavy skillet over high heat, then add the chicken and fry about 2 minutes on each side until well browned and the meat has started to caramelize.

Transfer the chicken to a roasting pan and roast 10 to 12 minutes until the juices run clear when the thickest part of the chicken is pierced with the tip of a sharp knife.

Meanwhile, heat the remaining oil in a large, heavy pot over medium-high heat. Add the bacon pieces and fry 3 to 4 minutes until crisp and golden brown. Add the cabbage and butter and cook 3 to 4 minutes longer, stirring, until the cabbage starts to soften. Add the wine and cream and bring to a boil.

Reduce the heat to low and simmer 5 to 6 minutes, stirring occasionally, until the mixture has reduced to a thick sauce. Stir in the chives. Spoon the sauce over the chicken and serve with mashed potatoes.

Serves 4
Preparation time: 10 minutes
Cooking time: 20 minutes

2 tablespoons peanut oil
4 chicken statler breasts or regular breasts, skin on
5½ ounces bacon, cut in pieces
10 ounces cabbage (about 7 cups), chopped
¼ cup cup unsalted butter
⅓ cup white wine
¾ cup heavy cream
2 tablespoons chopped chives
sea salt and freshly ground black pepper
1 recipe quantity Creamy Mashed Potatoes (see page 212), to serve

Chicken fricassee

Chicken fricassee is a very simple and delicate dish made up of small pieces of meat cooked in a light white sauce. It is important to use a good-quality chicken broth so make your own or buy some fresh, if you can, rather than using canned broth.

Melt half the butter in a skillet over low heat. Add the mushrooms and cook 5 minutes until just tender, then remove from the pan.

Add the remaining butter to the pan. Season the chicken with salt and pepper and add to the pan. Cook a few minutes on each side until sealed but without coloring the chicken.

Add the flour and cook 2 minutes, stirring continuously, then turn up the heat to medium and gradually add the broth, still stirring. Bring to a boil, then turn the heat down to low and simmer about 15 minutes until the chicken juices run clear when the thickest part of the chicken is pierced with the tip of a sharp knife.

Whisk together the egg yolk and cream with a pinch of salt in a bowl or measuring jug, then whisk in a ladleful of the hot broth. Stir the mixture into the skillet and season with a little salt and pepper. Add the cooked mushrooms and the parsley and simmer 5 minutes longer until piping hot and well blended.

Serve the chicken with buttered carrots.

Serves 4
Preparation time: 20 minutes,
  plus making the broth
Cooking time: 35 minutes

3½ tablespoons unsalted butter
3½ ounces button mushrooms
12 skinless boneless chicken thighs,
  cut into chunks
¼ cup all-purpose flour
2 cups Chicken Broth (see page 197)
1 egg yolk
3 tablespoons heavy cream
2 tablespoons chopped parsley leaves
sea salt and freshly ground black pepper
1 recipe quantity Buttered Carrots (see
  page 216), to serve

Spice-rubbed, roasted half-chicken with smoky-bacon french fries

Roast chicken is healthy, full of protein and a classic dish but it's hardly something new, so here is my modern take on roast chicken, adding a spicy rub that gives your taste buds a kick and makes sure you sit up and take notice. Plus, these are no ordinary french fries as they are sprinkled with my smoky-bacon crumb—different and delicious. You can keep the rub in an airtight container for a few days, so make it ahead of time to speed up an after-work meal.

Start soaking, then cooking the french fries, following steps 1 and 2 on page 213.

Meanwhile, mix together all the spice rub ingredients. Put the half-chickens in a roasting pan and rub the mixture all over. Cover and let marinate 20 minutes in the refrigerator.

To make the smoky bacon mix, heat the broiler to high, then broil the pancetta for about 5 minutes until very crisp. Drain well on paper towels, then let cool. Put in a small blender with the remaining smoky bacon mix ingredients and blitz to a fine powder.

Heat the oil in a ridged grill pan over high heat, add the chicken halves in batches and cook 2 to 3 minutes on each side until colored, then transfer to a roasting pan and roast 8 to 10 minutes until the juices run clear when the thickest part of the chicken is pierced with the tip of a sharp knife.

Meanwhile, finish cooking the french fries, following step 3 on page 213.

Season the french fries with a little salt, then sprinkle the smoky bacon crumb generously over the french fries. Serve the chicken with the smoky-bacon fries and coleslaw.

Serves 4
Preparation time: 30 minutes,
  plus 20 minutes marinating
Cooking time: 30 minutes

1 recipe quantity French Fries
  (see page 213)
1 tablespoon olive oil
4 half-chickens
sea salt and freshly ground black pepper
1 recipe quantity Celery Root & Carrot
  Coleslaw (see page 218), to serve

FOR THE SPICE RUB
2 tablespoons smoked paprika
1 tablespoon smoked sea salt or sea salt,
  finely ground
1 tablespoon sugar
1 tablespoon mustard powder
2 teaspoons chili powder
1 tablespoon ground cumin
1 tablespoon ground black pepper
1 tablespoon granulated garlic
1 tablespoon cayenne pepper

FOR THE SMOKY BACON MIX
8 strips of pancetta, chopped
1/2 teaspoon cayenne pepper
2 teaspoons smoked paprika
2 teaspoons dark brown sugar

Homemade crumpets with chicken & chive-scrambled eggs

Homemade crumpets are something a little bit special—I often used to eat them as a child with lots of butter. Most people wouldn't think of making them, but they are actually quite easy to make yourself—and even easier if you buy some crumpet rings from any kitchenware store, although if you don't have any, just use a 3-inch round cookie cutter. Crumpets go well with soft scrambled egg and fresh chives, making this a perfect little recipe for breakfast or brunch.

Heat the milk just to lukewarm in a pot over medium heat. Whisk in the yeast until dissolved. Mix together the flour, sugar and salt in a bowl, then gradually add the milk and yeast mixture, stirring continuously. Stir in ½ cup lukewarm water and whisk together until completely combined. Cover with plastic wrap and let it rise 1½ hours in a warm place.

Stir the baking powder and half the oil into the batter mix. Heat the remaining oil in a nonstick skillet over medium-high heat and use a piece of paper towel to grease the pan. Also grease with oil, or cold water, the inside of as many crumpet rings as will fit in the pan, then put the rings in the pan. Pour some of the batter into each ring, filling them three-quarters full, and cook 2 minutes, then turn the heat down to low and cook 3 minutes longer until the tops are drying out and have a few holes. Flip the crumpets over, using a spatula, and cook 1 to 2 minutes longer. Remove from the pan and set them on a wire rack while you cook the remaining crumpets.

Meanwhile, to make the scrambled eggs, whisk together the eggs and chives in a pot over medium heat. Add the shredded chicken and season with salt and pepper. Cook 4 to 5 minutes, stirring every 30 to 60 seconds to stop the eggs overcooking. Stir in the butter and serve immediately with the warm crumpets.

Serves 4
Preparation time: 15 minutes, plus 1½ hours rising
Cooking time: 15 minutes

FOR THE CRUMPETS
¾ cup milk
1 tablespoon fresh yeast or 1½ teaspoons dried yeast
1¾ cups all-purpose flour
2 teaspoons sugar
1 teaspoon salt
2 teaspoons baking powder
2 tablespoons olive oil

FOR THE CHIVE-SCRAMBLED EGGS
10 eggs, beaten
3 tablespoons chopped chives
1 smoked chicken breast (see page 23), shredded
2 tablespoons unsalted butter
sea salt and freshly ground black pepper

Chicken huevos rancheros

Bring a bit of Mexican flavor into your kitchen with this tasty dish of refried beans with all the trimmings. If you like your food spicy, you can increase the amount of chili you add to the dish. If you are short of time, simply serve with a store-bought guacamole.

Heat the butter and half the oil in a large skillet over medium heat, add the onion and garlic and fry about 4 minutes until soft.

Add the chorizo, bacon and chicken, and fry 5 minutes, stirring, until colored and just cooked through. Add the refried beans and tomatoes. Stir in the chili, jalapeño pepper and cilantro and season with salt and pepper to taste. Cook 10 minutes longer until all the ingredients are hot and well blended.

Meanwhile, in a separate skillet, heat the remaining oil and fry the eggs until the yolks are just cooked. Slide the eggs on top of the chicken mixture and sprinkle with the shredded cheese. Serve the huevos rancheros hot with the guacamole.

Serves 4
Preparation time: 15 minutes
Cooking time: 20 minutes

1 tablespoon butter
2 tablespoons olive oil
1 onion, finely chopped
1 garlic clove, chopped
2 ounces chorizo, chopped
1 thick smoked bacon strip, cut into pieces
¾ cup ground chicken
1⅔ cups refried beans
1 cup canned crushed tomatoes
½ red chili, seeded and chopped
1 jalapeño pepper, seeded and chopped
¼ cup chopped cilantro leaves
4 large eggs
3 tablespoons shredded cheddar cheese
sea salt and freshly ground black pepper
1 recipe quantity Guacamole
  (see page 201), to serve

Chicken Niçoise with caper & roasted-tomato dressing

I began with a classic Niçoise salad but this one has my own little twists—a steamed chicken breast to keep it nice and healthy, a tomato dressing made with capers to give it definition, and a delicious sprinkling of olive crumb on the top.

Heat the oven to 275°F. Reserve a few olives and bake the remainder for 30 minutes until dried out, then let cool and chop finely.

Meanwhile, put a large pot of water on to simmer, with a steamer insert on top. Season the chicken with salt and pepper, then put it into the steamer, cover and cook 20 to 25 minutes until the juices run clear when the thickest part of the chicken is pierced with the tip of a sharp knife.

At the same time, put the potatoes in a pot of cold water and bring to a boil over high heat, then turn the heat down to low and simmer 10 minutes until tender, then drain. Bring a small pot of water to a boil over high heat, add the green beans and cook 2 minutes. Drain, then run the beans under ice-cold water to stop them from cooking any further. Drain, then set aside.

Meanwhile, bring a pot of water to a boil over high heat. Gently lower the eggs into the water, then boil 6½ minutes. Lift the eggs out of the water, using a slotted spoon, place in a bowl of ice-cold water to stop them from cooking any further and let cool 5 minutes. Peel in the water, to stop them from breaking, then drain.

Grind the peppercorns and salt in a spice grinder or mortar and pestle, then tip into a shallow bowl. Roll the peeled egg in the mixture. Whisk together the dressing ingredients in a bowl, then season with salt and pepper.

Slice the chicken and cut the eggs in half, then put on top of the green beans, potatoes and olive halves. Drizzle with the dressing and finish with a few pinches of olive crumb.

Serves 4
Preparation time: 20 minutes, plus making the slow-roasted tomatoes
Cooking time: 30 minutes

½ cup pitted ripe or green olives, cut in half
4 skinless chicken breasts
14 ounces baby new potatoes
5½ ounces fine green beans
4 eggs
2 tablespoons black peppercorns
1 teaspoon sea salt

FOR THE CAPER & ROASTED TOMATO DRESSING
½ cup Slow-Roasted Tomatoes (see page 218)
2 tablespoons drained capers, rinsed
2 tablespoons red wine vinegar or raspberry vinegar
⅓ cup olive oil

Chicken, lemongrass & thyme Scotch eggs with mustard mayonnaise

This is one of the dishes I mastered over the years of running a pub, although these are no ordinary Scotch eggs because I've brought in Far Eastern flavors to bring a new perspective to this British dish. I use the eggs from my mother-in-law's cage-free hens and encase the eggs with their bright and runny yolks in moist, flavorsome meat with a lovely crisp crumb.

Heat the oven to 400°F. Bring a pan of water to a boil over high heat. Gently lower the eggs into the water, then boil 6½ minutes. Lift the eggs out, using a slotted spoon, put in a bowl of ice-cold water to stop them from cooking further and leave for 5 minutes. Peel them in the water, to stop them from breaking, then drain and let cool.

Meanwhile, mix together the meat-coating ingredients, seasoning them with salt and pepper. Put the flour and the breadcrumbs in two separate shallow bowls. In a third bowl, whisk together the eggs and milk and season with a pinch of salt to make an egg wash.

Roll the hard-boiled eggs in the flour. Dust your hands with a little more flour and pat out one-quarter of the chicken mixture into a flat oval on your hand. Put a boiled egg in the center and gently wrap the meat around the egg so that it is evenly covered, pinching the edges together to seal. Roll the egg in the egg wash, shaking off any excess, then roll it in the breadcrumbs, then roll it in the egg wash and breadcrumbs again. Repeat with the remaining eggs.

Heat the oil in a deep, heavy pot to 325°F, when a cube of bread browns in 60 seconds. Gently lower the eggs into the oil, using a slotted spoon, and cook 8 to 10 minutes, turning occasionally, until the breadcrumbs are a dark golden brown. Remove from the oil and drain on paper towels 2 to 3 minutes, then transfer to the oven for 10 minutes to ensure that the chicken is cooked through but the outside is not too brown. Mix the mustard into the mayonnaise. Cut the eggs in half and serve with the flavored mayonnaise and a fresh salad.

Serves 4
Preparation time: 30 minutes, plus making the mayonnaise
Cooking time: 25 minutes

4 large eggs
sunflower oil, for deep-frying
1 teaspoon Dijon mustard
⅔ cup Mayonnaise (see page 202)
1 recipe quantity Green Salad (see page 219), to serve

FOR THE CHICKEN & THYME COATING
14 ounces ground chicken
1 lemongrass stalk, finely chopped
leaves from 2 thyme sprigs, finely chopped
grated zest and juice of 1 lemon
sea salt and freshly ground black pepper

FOR THE BREADCRUMB COATING
¼ cup all-purpose flour
1 cup panko breadcrumbs or fine dried breadcrumbs
4 eggs
½ cup milk

Chicken & scallion patties with red onion, tomato & cilantro salad

A light and healthy recipe, these neat little patties make a lovely simple snack that can be served as an appetizer, canapé or even a light lunch. Team them with any fresh salad ingredients to vary things, or add a few french fries or buttered new potatoes to make a more substantial meal.

Mix together all the ingredients for the patties, cover with plastic wrap and chill 30 minutes in the refrigerator.

Shape the chicken mixture into 8 small burgers. Heat the frying oils in a skillet until shimmering, then add the patties and fry 2 minutes on each side until cooked through and golden. Drain on paper towels.

Meanwhile, mix together the salad ingredients, adding a little dressing to taste. Serve the patties with the fresh onion, tomato and herb salad.

Serves 4
Preparation time: 15 minutes, plus 30 minutes chilling, and making the dressing
Cooking time: 5 minutes

FOR THE CHICKEN & SCALLION PATTIES
14 ounces ground chicken
4 scallions, finely chopped
1 tablespoon light soy sauce
2 tablespoons chopped cilantro leaves
1 tablespoon sesame oil
1 garlic clove, finely chopped
1 teaspoon Worcestershire sauce
2 tablespoons peeled and grated ginger root
2 tablespoons sesame seeds
1 red chili, seeded and finely chopped

2 tablespoons olive oil, for frying
1 teaspoon sesame oil, for frying

FOR THE ONION, TOMATO & CILANTRO SALAD
2 red onions, thinly sliced
2 tablespoons chopped cilantro leaves
3 vine tomatoes, finely chopped
sea salt and freshly ground black pepper
a drizzle of Bean House Salad Dressing (see page 203)

Curried chicken turnovers with mango chutney

At home in the UK, we call these pasties —flavorsome meat and vegetables surrounded in a flaky, well-cooked pastry and, of course, served with a sauce or chutney. The recipe makes eight small turnovers but you could make four large ones, if you prefer.

To make the dough, put the flour, salt and sugar in a bowl, then rub in the butter, using your fingertips, until the mixture resembles coarse breadcrumbs. Stir in 1 egg and about 1 tablespoon water, if necessary, a drop at a time, to bind the ingredients together. Roll into a ball, wrap in plastic wrap and chill in the refrigerator while you make the filling.

Melt the butter in a skillet over medium heat. Add the onion and curry paste and fry about 3 minutes until the onions are soft but not brown. Add the carrot and cook 2 minutes. Toss the chicken with the cornstarch to coat, then add to the pan and fry 2 to 3 minutes longer, stirring, until the chicken is just colored.

Add the corn and broth, stirring until it comes to a boil. Turn the heat down to low and cook 2 to 3 minutes more until the chicken is cooked through. Add the cream and cook a few minutes longer until the sauce thickens. Season with salt and pepper to taste, then remove from the heat and set aside to cool.

Heat the oven to 400°F and grease a baking sheet. Roll out the dough on a lightly floured surface and cut out 4 large or 8 small equal-size circles. Spoon the filling into the center of each circle. Mix the remaining egg with 1 tablespoon water to make an egg wash and brush this around the edges of the dough, then bring both sides to meet at the top to contain the chicken mixture. Crimp the top to seal the turnovers by pushing the dough between the index finger of one hand against the index finger and thumb of the other hand. Put on the prepared baking sheet and bake 8 to 10 minutes, then brush with the remaining egg wash and return to the oven for 8 to 10 minutes longer until golden.

Serve the turnovers with mango chutney and a fresh salad.

Serves 4
Preparation time: 30 minutes, plus
  making the curry paste and broth
Cooking time: 35 minutes

FOR THE DOUGH
2 cups all-purpose flour, plus extra for
  dusting
a pinch salt
1/2 teaspoon sugar
1/2 cup cold unsalted butter, cut into small
  pieces
2 eggs

FOR THE CURRIED CHICKEN FILLING
3 1/2 tablespoons unsalted butter, plus
  extra for greasing
1 onion, finely chopped
1 tablespoon Curry Paste (see page 204)
1 carrot, peeled and finely chopped
2 skinless chicken breasts, cubed
1 teaspoon cornstarch
1 cup drained canned corn kernels
scant 1 cup Chicken Broth (see page 197)
1/2 cup heavy cream
sea salt and freshly ground black pepper

1/4 cup Mango Chutney (see page 206)
1 recipe quantity Herb Salad
  (see page 219)

Chicken & sesame shrimp toasts

I've always been a fan of sesame shrimp toast, especially when served with homemade sweet and sour chili sauce like the one I serve with my Vietnamese-style wraps (see page 161). But the addition of the chicken just lifts it to another level, as the chicken and shrimp work really well together. It makes a great snack or a delicious appetizer.

Heat the oven to 400°F. Put the shrimp, chicken, ginger, soy sauce, scallions, sesame oil and a pinch of salt in a blender and blitz to a paste. Spoon the paste onto the slices of baguette to make a nice mound in the center, leaving a small space around the edge. Put the baguette slices on a plate and sprinkle liberally with the sesame seeds, covering the shrimp paste.

Heat the oil in a large skillet over medium heat, add the slices, paste-side down, and fry 2 to 3 minutes until just golden brown, then flip over and fry the other sides 2 minutes longer.

Transfer to a baking sheet and roast 2 to 3 minutes to dry out. Let cool before serving.

Serves 4
Preparation time: 15 minutes
Cooking time: 10 minutes

5½ ounces raw peeled tiger shrimp
1 skinless boneless chicken thigh
1 tablespoon peeled and finely chopped
  ginger root
1 tablespoon soy sauce
1 tablespoon chopped scallions
1 teaspoon sesame oil
a pinch salt
12 slices of baguette, ideally a few days old
  and slightly dry
¼ cup sesame seeds
⅔ cup peanut oil
sea salt

Sticky barbecued chicken wings

There are times when you don't really want a big meal, but prefer to graze on smaller, easy-to-eat items, and these barbecued wings definitely fit the bill. For best results, make your own coleslaw, if you have the time, then you know it is fresh and crunchy.

Mix together all the marinade ingredients in a bowl until well blended. Stir in the chicken wings, making sure they are completely coated. Cover with plastic wrap and let marinate 2 to 3 hours, or ideally overnight, in the refrigerator.

Heat the oven to 400°F. Spread the chicken wings evenly in a large roasting pan, pouring any excess marinade over the chicken. Roast 20 to 30 minutes until the wings are cooked through and the marinade has caramelized so it is nice and sticky. Serve warm on their own or with coleslaw.

Serves 4
Preparation time: 15 minutes,
 plus at least 2 hours marinating
Cooking time: 30 minutes

12 chicken wings
1 recipe quantity Celery Root & Carrot
 Coleslaw (see page 218), to serve

FOR THE STICKY BARBECUE MARINADE
3 tablespoons ketchup
1½ tablespoons soy sauce
1½ teaspoons smoked paprika
1 teaspoon smoked sea salt or sea salt
1½ tablespoons honey
2 garlic cloves, finely chopped
1¼-inch piece ginger root, peeled and
 finely chopped
2 tablespoons peanut oil

Chicken tacos with tomato salsa & guacamole

Mexican food has a great balance of fresh, spicy and fragrant flavors with lots of cilantro in most recipes. I really like tacos and find them a quick and easy meal to make for friends, which is great for keeping everything nice and relaxed. Since you can make most of this recipe ahead of time, you've got more time to enjoy with your friends—and a bottle or two of Mexican beer.

Heat the oil in a large pan over medium heat. Add the garlic, onion and red pepper, and fry 2 to 3 minutes until just soft. Add the chicken and cook 3 to 4 minutes, stirring, until the chicken is just starting to color. Add the dry spices and mix everything together well, then add the chicken broth and bring to a boil. Turn the heat down to low, cover and simmer 15 to 20 minutes, stirring every 5 minutes, until the liquid has evaporated and the chicken is browned and cooked through.

While the chicken is cooking, make the tomato salsa and the guacamole, and heat the oven to 350°F. Warm the tacos in the oven 2 to 3 minutes so they are all ready when your chicken is cooked.

Fill the tacos with the chicken mixture and top with spoonfuls of tomato salsa and guacamole. Sprinkle with shredded cheese and serve with the lime wedges.

Serves 4
Preparation time: 10 minutes, plus
  making the broth, salsa and guacamole
Cooking time: 30 minutes

1 tablespoon olive oil
2 garlic cloves, finely chopped
1 onion, finely chopped
1 red bell pepper, seeded and finely
  chopped
2¼ cups ground chicken
1 teaspoon smoked paprika
½ teaspoon chili powder
½ teaspoon ground cumin
1 teaspoon ground coriander
1 cup Chicken Broth (see page 197)
1 recipe quantity Tomato Salsa
  (see page 201)
1 recipe quantity Guacamole
  (see page 201)
16 taco shells
1 cup shredded sharp cheddar cheese
1 lime, cut into wedges

Hazelnut, chicken & tarragon empanadas

Empanadas are small, savory turnovers, common in Spain and Mexico. They come with all different fillings and there are even empanada festivals in Spain, championing the regional specialties. I've chosen to partner the chicken with the strong, sharp flavor of tarragon with soft mushrooms and toasted hazelnuts—or cobnuts as I call them—for that extra bit of texture, and I've wrapped that delicious combination in a crisp short pastry crust.

Melt the butter in a large pan over medium heat. Add the onion and garlic and fry 3 to 4 minutes until softened. Add the mushrooms and cook 2 minutes longer, then add the ground chicken and cook about 5 minutes, stirring, until just browned.

Add the broth, then the tarragon, and simmer 5 minutes to reduce the liquid, then add the cream and simmer gently 5 minutes longer.

Add the spinach and hazelnuts, season with salt and pepper to taste, and stir everything together well. Transfer to a bowl and let cool slightly, then cover with plastic wrap and chill about 30 minutes in the refrigerator until the mixture firms up slightly.

Heat the oven to 400°F and line a baking sheet with baking parchment. Divide the dough into 8 equal pieces, then roll out one piece at a time on a lightly floured surface into a circle about ⅛ inch thick. Spoon one eighth of the cold meat mixture into the center. Brush the edges of the dough circle with a little cold water, then fold half of the dough over the top and seal the edges together by pressing with the tines of a fork. Repeat the process to make 8 empanadas.

Place the sealed empanadas on a baking sheet. Beat the egg with 1 tablespoon water and brush it over the empanadas, then bake 10 minutes until golden brown.

Serve hot or cold, with a fresh salad.

Serves 4
Preparation time: 30 minutes, plus 30 minutes chilling, and making the broth and pastry dough
Cooking time: 30 minutes

3 tablespoons unsalted butter
1 onion, thinly sliced
1 garlic clove, chopped
4 ounces crimini mushrooms, quartered
1 heaped cup ground chicken
½ cup Chicken Broth (see page 197)
1 tablespoon chopped tarragon leaves
⅓ cup heavy cream
½ cup spinach leaves, chopped
heaped 1 cup toasted hazelnuts, roughly chopped
1 recipe quantity Pastry Dough (see page 208)
a little flour, for dusting
1 egg
sea salt and freshly ground black pepper
1 recipe quantity Green Salad (see page 219) or a mixed salad, to serve

Chicken corn dogs

Corn dogs are an all-American classic street food, traditionally made with a hotdog dipped in a batter and deep-fried. Here I've made them with chicken sausages, because the tasty chicken and pancetta filling works so well with the crisp coating. Why not include them in your 4th of July offerings—they'll be sure to be popular with the whole family.

Put 8 wooden skewers in a bowl of cold water to soak for 1 hour. Put all the sauce ingredients in a pot over high heat and bring to a boil. Turn the heat down to low, cover the pan and simmer about 30 minutes, or until the sauce is rich and thick, stirring occasionally and adding a little more water if the sauce becomes too dry. Leave it chunky or puree in a blender for a smooth sauce.

Meanwhile, mix together the cornmeal, flour, sugar, nutmeg and baking powder, add the eggs and milk and whisk together to form thick batter. Season with salt and pepper. Pour the batter into a straight pint glass.

Heat the oil in a deep, heavy pot to 350°F, when a cube of day-old bread will brown in 40 seconds. Thread the skewers lengthwise through the sausages.

Dip the first sausage into the glass with the batter until coated, then slowly lift it out and submerge it in the hot oil, turning occasionally for 3 to 4 minutes until browned. Remove from the oil, drain on paper towels for 1 minute, then keep them warm while you cook the remaining corn dogs. Serve with the barbecue sauce.

Serves 4
Preparation time: 15 minutes, plus making the sausages
Cooking time: 20 minutes

1 cup cornmeal or polenta
1 cup self-rising flour
2½ tablespoons sugar
a small pinch of grated nutmeg
2 teaspoons baking powder
1 egg
scant 1 cup 2% milk
peanut oil, for deep-frying
8 cooked Chicken & Pancetta Sausages (see page 120)
sea salt and freshly ground black pepper

FOR THE BARBECUE SAUCE
1 x 15-ounce can tomato puree
1 teaspoon smoked paprika
1 tablespoon fresh apple juice
2 tablespoons balsamic vinegar
1 tablespoon Worcestershire sauce
scant ½ cup dark brown sugar
1 tablespoon ketchup
a few drops of Tabasco

Pulled chicken buns with barbecue sauce

There's something a bit special about pulled meat and barbecue sauce, and the combination works well with shredded chicken and my spicy sauce. A perfect snack for when friends drop by unannounced, you can make the sauce ahead of time and keep it in a sterilized airtight container in the refrigerator for up to 2 weeks.

Heat the oil in a large, nonstick pan over medium heat. Add the onion and garlic and fry 2 to 3 minutes until softened. Add all the remaining ingredients, except the buns, bring to a boil, then cover with a lid, turn down the heat to low and let simmer 1 hour until the chicken is cooked through and the sauce is thick, stirring occasionally. If it gets a bit dry, add 3 to 4 tablespoons water.

Lift out the chicken from the sauce and shred the meat, using two forks. Blitz the sauce in a blender until smooth, then strain it through a fine mesh strainer.

To assemble the burger buns, mix together some chicken and sauce and pile it into the buns. Serve with french fries and salad, if you like.

Serves 4
Preparation time: 20 minutes
Cooking time: 1 hour 5 minutes

1 tablespoon olive oil
1 onion, finely chopped
2 garlic cloves, finely chopped
2 skinless chicken breasts, sliced in half horizontally
2 skinless boneless chicken thighs
1 x 15-ounce can tomato puree
1 teaspoon smoked paprika
1 tablespoon fresh apple juice
2 tablespoons balsamic vinegar
1 tablespoon Worcestershire sauce
scant ½ cup dark brown sugar
1 tablespoon ketchup
a few drops of Tabasco
4 white or brown burger buns, sliced in half
sea salt and freshly ground black pepper
1 recipe quantity French Fries (see page 213), to serve
a mixed salad (optional), to serve

Chicken, cranberry & Stilton pie

Mix together the flour, salt and pepper in a bowl and make a well in the center. Melt the lard and butter in a pot with ⅔ cup water over low heat, then pour it into the flour. Add the egg yolk and use your hands to mix to a dough. Cover with a clean cloth and let cool 5 minutes, then cover with plastic wrap and leave it 20 minutes until cool enough to work.

Put the chicken in a pan and just cover with water. Bring to a boil over medium heat, then turn the heat down to low, cover with a lid and cook 12 minutes until the juices run clear when the thickest part of the chicken is pierced with the tip of a sharp knife. Drain and set aside to dry.

Heat the oven to 425°F. Put a cookie sheet in the oven to heat up and grease a springform cake tin. I use a 6¼-inch tin but you can use an 8-inch tin to make a shallower pie. Mix together the chicken, bacon, cranberries, Stilton, thyme and parsley, and season with salt and pepper.

Break off about one-quarter of the dough, then roll out the remainder on a lightly floured surface to a circle large enough to use to line the base and side of the prepared tin. Fill with the meat mixture. Roll out the remaining dough into a circle large enough for the top of the pie. Brush the edge of the base with water and seal the lid on top by crimping the pastry edges together with a fork. Make a small hole in the center. Mix the egg and milk and brush it over the top. Roll and cut the trimmings to decorate the top, then brush again.

Put the pie on the hot cookie sheet and bake about 20 minutes, then turn the oven down to 315°F and bake 1½ hours longer until golden brown. Cover with foil if it browns too quickly.

Bring the broth to just below a simmer in a pan, then remove from the heat and whisk in the gelatin. Slowly pour the hot broth into the hole in the pie, stopping when it reaches the top. Let cool, then chill 2 hours in the refrigerator. Serve with spiced apple chutney.

Serves 8
Preparation time: 30 minutes, plus cooling, 2 hours chilling, and making the broth
Cooking time: 2 hours 10 minutes

FOR THE PASTRY DOUGH

3⅓ cups plus 1 tablespoon all-purpose flour, plus extra for dusting
2 teaspoons fine sea salt
1 tablespoon freshly ground black pepper
1 cup minus 1 tablespoon shortening
3½ tablespoons unsalted butter, plus extra for greasing
1 egg yolk
1 egg, lightly beaten
1 teaspoon milk

FOR THE CHICKEN, CRANBERRY & STILTON FILLING

2 skinless chicken breasts, cut in half horizontally
10½ ounces skinless boneless chicken thighs, cut into ½- to ¾-inch pieces
1 strip cooked Canadian bacon, finely chopped
1⅔ cups cranberries, thawed if frozen
½ cup crumbled Stilton cheese
1 tablespoon chopped thyme leaves
1 tablespoon chopped parsley leaves
scant 1 cup Chicken Broth (see page 197)
2 teaspoons powdered gelatin
sea salt and freshly ground black pepper

Spiced Apple Chutney (see page 206), to serve

Chicken, leek & ham pie with tarragon crust

Growing up in pubs was great—especially since Mom always had a meat pie on the menu. I've given this chicken and leek pie my little twist by adding some ham hock and making it with a tarragon puff pastry crust. You can't go wrong with a great pie to impress your guests.

Roll out the pastry on a lightly floured surface, sprinkle with ½ tablespoon of the tarragon and roll it in before folding. Repeat on the following turns until all the tarragon is added to the pastry. Chill as directed.

While the pastry is chilling, heat the oil in a skillet over medium heat. Add the chicken and cook 2 to 3 minutes on each side until just cooked. Remove from the skillet and set aside. Wipe the skillet clean, then return it to medium heat. Add the butter, then the garlic and leeks and fry 2 to 4 minutes until softened.

Sprinkle over the flour, then gradually begin to add the broth, whisking continuously so it doesn't form lumps, until you have added all the broth and the liquid has thickened slightly. It should take 4 to 5 minutes. Stir in the cream, then the chicken, ham and tarragon. Season with salt and pepper to taste. Remove from the heat and leave to cool slightly.

Heat the oven to 400°F and grease a 9½-inch pie dish with butter. Roll out the pastry to twice the size of the pie dish, then use half to line the base, trimming the edges so the pastry just sits on the rim of the dish. Spoon in the filling. Brush the edge of the pastry with a little water, then put the remaining pastry on top. Trim the edges and crimp the top and bottom together to seal the pie by pressing with the tines of a fork.

Cut a small hole in the top of the pastry to allow the steam escape. Beat the egg with 1 tablespoon water to make an egg wash, then brush it over the top of the pie. Bake 30 to 40 minutes until the pastry is a lovely golden brown. Serve with buttered new potatoes and seasonal vegetables.

Serves 4
Preparation time: 30 minutes, plus at least 30 minutes chilling, and making the pastry dough and broth
Cooking time: 50 minutes

FOR THE PASTRY DOUGH

2 recipe quantities Rough Puff Pastry (see page 208), prepared to the first chilling
a little flour, for dusting
¼ cup chopped tarragon leaves
1 egg

FOR THE CHICKEN, LEEK & HAM FILLING

1 tablespoon olive oil
6 skinless boneless chicken thighs, cut into ¾-inch pieces
¼ cup unsalted butter, plus extra for greasing
2 garlic cloves, finely chopped
2 leeks, trimmed and thinly sliced
scant ½ cup all-purpose flour
scant 2 cups Chicken Broth (see page 197)
⅔ cup heavy cream
6 ounces cooked ham hock, shredded
1 tablespoon chopped tarragon leaves
sea salt and freshly ground black pepper

boiled and buttered new potatoes and seasonal vegetables, to serve

Chicken quiche lorraine

With the delicate balance of crisp pastry and soft egg filling, quiche makes a great light lunch, served hot or cold. But please, no soggy bottoms—bake the pie shell blind before filling. If you have any leftover filling, pour it into buttered ramekins and cook for half the time.

Sift the flour into a bowl, then rub in the butter with your fingertips until the mixture resembles breadcrumbs. Make a well in the center, add 1 egg and mix everything together to a dough, adding 1 tablespoon water, if needed. Roll out on a lightly floured surface until smooth. Wrap in plastic wrap and chill 10 minutes in the refrigerator.

Heat the oil in a skillet over medium-high heat. Add the chicken and stir-fry 3 to 4 minutes until cooked through. Remove from the pan and set aside.

Heat the oven to 350°F, put a cookie sheet in the oven to heat up and grease an 8-inch removable-bottomed fluted tart tin. Roll out the pastry on a lightly floured surface to ³⁄₈-inch thick and use to line the prepared tin. Prick the base with a fork to stop the pastry from rising. Line with a double layer of plastic wrap, then fill with dry rice. Put on the hot baking sheet and bake 12 minutes, then remove the plastic wrap and rice.

Whisk together the milk and remaining egg to make an egg wash and brush this over the crust, then return it to the oven for 10 minutes until golden. Set aside to cool, then chill 15 minutes in the refrigerator.

To make the filling, melt the butter in a pan over medium heat, add the onion and bacon and fry 5 minutes until golden. Spoon it into the crust, top with the chicken and sprinkle with the cheese. Whisk together the cream, milk and eggs, and season with a little salt and pepper. Pour in enough mixture to fill the pastry case.

Bake 15 to 20 minutes until the filling is golden and set. If the pastry starts to go too dark, turn the oven down to 315°F. Serve the quiche warm on its own, or with celery root rémoulade or salad.

Serves 6 to 8
Preparation time: 30 minutes, plus 25 minutes chilling and cooling
Cooking time: 50 minutes

FOR THE PASTRY DOUGH
scant 2 cups all-purpose flour, plus extra for dusting
1¼ cups cold unsalted butter, cubed
2 eggs
1 tablespoon milk

FOR THE EGG & BACON FILLING
1 tablespoon olive oil
1 skinless chicken breast, finely chopped
2 tablespoons unsalted butter, plus extra for greasing
1 onion, finely chopped
2 thick strips Canadian bacon, finely chopped
1 cup shredded extra sharp strong cheddar, such as Snowdonia Cheese Black Bomber
¾ cup heavy cream
⅓ cup milk
2 large eggs
sea salt and freshly ground black pepper

1 recipe quantity Celery Root Rémoulade (see page 217) or 1 recipe quantity Green Salad (see page 219), to serve

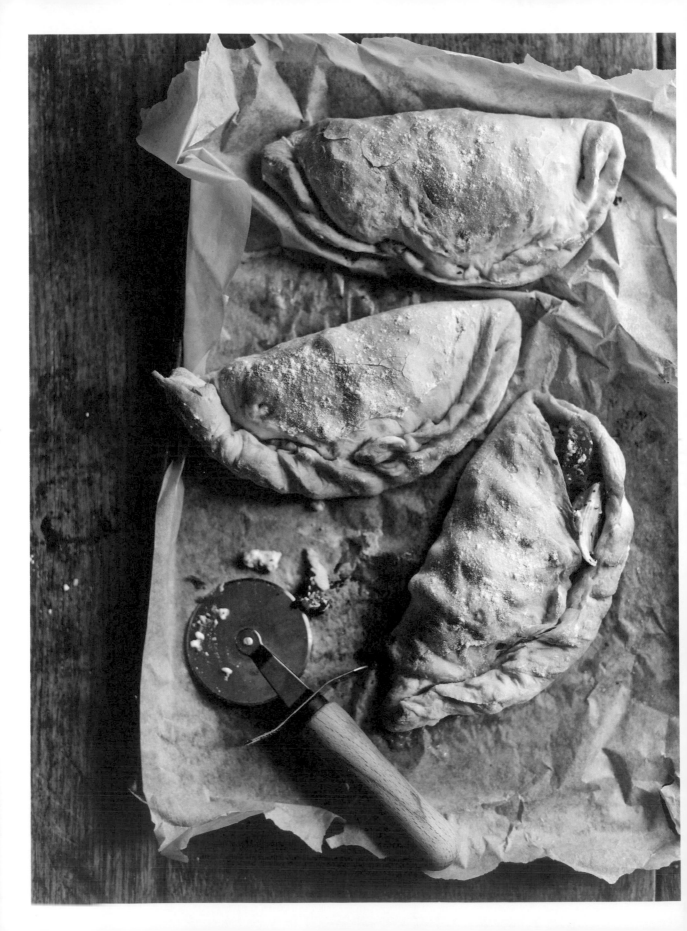

Chicken, cherry tomato, spinach & feta calzone

I'm sure you'll agree we all love pizza, and a calzone is like a stuffed turnover made with pizza dough pasty. Serve them like this with a salad to make a delicious main meal, or make eight calzone instead of four and serve them as a handy snack that will fill you up for a few hours. Try experimenting with all sorts of ingredients the next time you make them.

Heat the oven to 400°F and line 2 baking sheets with parchment paper. Put the chicken in a roasting tray and roast 12 to 15 minutes until the juices run clear when the thickest part of the chicken is pierced with the tip of a sharp knife. Let stand 5 minutes, then cut into small pieces.

Cut the pizza dough into quarters and roll out each piece on a lightly floured surface into a circle about ½ inch thick. Put the circles on the prepared baking sheets.

Mix together the cooked chicken and all the remaining ingredients, season with salt and pepper, and gently toss together. Divide the filling among the pizza dough circles. Brush the edges of the circles with a little cold water, then fold half of the dough over the top and seal the edges together by twisting the dough.

Bake about 15 minutes until golden. Serve warm or cold, with a fresh salad.

Serves 4
Preparation time: 20 minutes,
  plus making the dough
Cooking time: 30 minutes

2 skinless chicken breasts, quartered
½ recipe quantity Pizza Dough (see page 207)
a little flour, for dusting
1½ cups chopped feta cheese
1½ cups baby cherry tomatoes
1 tablespoon chopped lovage or cilantro leaves
1 cup baby spinach leaves
2 tablespoons olive oil
sea salt and freshly ground black pepper
1 recipe quantity Microleaf & Carrot Salad (see page 219), to serve

Spinach & chicken ravioli with tomato sauce

Ravioli is a great combination of fresh pasta with, in this case, a meat filling, and I am serving it with a lovely rich sauce. Making fresh pasta is such a great technique to learn and it is so easy to do. If you like, you can make the ravioli ahead of time. Once sealed, you can freeze it before cooking, then simply cook it from frozen, making it really convenient for those looking for a nutritious meal in minutes.

Roll out the pasta on a lightly floured surface as thinly as possible, or use a pasta machine.

Heat the oil in a skillet over medium-high heat. Add the chicken and fry 4 to 5 minutes, stirring, until browned and cooked. Set aside to cool.

Rinse and drain the spinach, then put it in a pot with just the water clinging to the leaves. Place over medium heat until softened, then drain and tip into a bowl to cool slightly. Add the chicken and the remaining stuffing ingredients to the bowl and mix until combined.

Spoon the mixture into a pastry bag with a small, plain tip and pipe small round piles about the size of a cherry in rows over half the pasta sheet, leaving about 1½-inch gap between each one. Dampen the dough between the piles of filling, then fold the other half of the pasta over to create a top sheet, carefully sealing between the ravioli and making sure you don't create any air pockets. Cut out the ravioli, using a 1½-inch cookie cutter, pressing together the edges to seal.

Bring a large pot of water to a boil over high heat, add the ravioli, in batches if necessary, and return to a boil. Simmer about 6 minutes until just tender. Drain well.

Meanwhile, put the tomato sauce in a pot over medium heat and bring to a boil, stirring to make sure it is heated through. Add the ravioli and toss together to serve.

Serves 4
Preparation time: 30 minutes,
  plus making the dough and sauce
Cooking time: 20 minutes

1 recipe quantity Fresh Egg Pasta
  (see page 207)
a little flour, for dusting
1 recipe quantity Tomato Sauce
  (see page 199)

FOR THE STUFFING
2 tablespoons olive oil
1¾ cups ground chicken
1¾ cups spinach leaves
3 tablespoons unsalted butter,
  at room temperature
2 eggs
½ cup shredded sharp cheese
2 tablespoons chopped chives
sea salt and freshly ground black pepper

Stuffed chicken thighs & egg noodles in cider cream

Succulent poached chicken and soft noodles bathed in a creamy cider sauce make a wonderful comfort dish—and it's so easy to make. If you can plan ahead, make the stuffed thighs ahead of time since you can keep them wrapped in the refrigerator for a day or two before you cook them.

Mix together the ground chicken and parsley in a bowl and season with salt and pepper. Lay a double layer of plastic wrap on the counter and put one of the chicken thighs in the center. Open out the chicken thigh and put one-eighth of the ground meat mixture down the center, then roll the thigh to encase the stuffing and tie in three places. Roll the plastic wrap around the chicken, pushing out any air as you do so, and tie each end securely in a knot. Wrap in the same way with aluminum foil. Repeat with the remaining thighs.

Bring a pot of water to a boil over high heat. Put the chicken bundles into the water, turn the heat down to low and simmer 10 minutes. Remove and set aside. Meanwhile, bring a large pot of water to a boil over high heat, add the noodles and boil 4 minutes until soft. Drain, then drizzle with the oil and keep warm.

To make the cider cream, melt the butter in a pot over low heat. Add the shallots and cook 2 minutes until soft, then stir in the flour and cook 2 minutes. Gradually add the cider, whisking continuously to stop any lumps from forming, then gradually whisk in the broth and bring to a simmer. Add the thyme and cook about 5 minutes, then add the cream and season with salt and pepper. Remove from the heat, cover and set aside.

Melt the butter in a large skillet as you unwrap the thighs. Add them to the pan and fry 1 to 2 minutes on each side until browned, in batches if necessary.

Add the noodles to the skillet with a few spoonfuls of the sauce and warm them through. Slice the chicken thickly and serve on a bed of noodles with some extra cider cream spooned over. Serve with crusty bread.

Serves 4
Preparation time: 30 minutes,
　plus making the broth
Cooking time: 25 minutes

7 ounces ground chicken
2 tablespoons chopped parsley leaves
8 skinless boneless chicken thighs
10½ ounces egg noodles
1 tablespoon olive oil
1 tablespoon unsalted butter
sea salt and freshly ground black pepper
crusty bread, to serve

FOR THE CIDER CREAM
1¾ ounces unsalted butter
2 shallots, finely chopped
¼ cup all-purpose flour
scant ½ cup hard cider
1¾ cups Chicken Broth (see page 197)
1 thyme sprig
3 tablespoons heavy cream

Chicken & butternut squash gnocchi with sage butter

The first time I had gnocchi was when I went snowboarding in the Alps—it's the ideal dish for active people as it's a great source of carbs to give you plenty of energy for the snowy slopes. I wanted to try a different spin on traditional gnocchi and as I really like the texture of butternut squash, I decided to add that to the chicken to make a dumpling. For this recipe, I have teamed the gnocchi with mushrooms and greens, but they would go equally well with one of my sauces, such as Fresh Basil Pesto (see page 201), or on their own as an appetizer for six.

Heat the oven to 400°F. Put the butternut squash on a baking sheet, drizzle with the oil, cover with aluminum foil and bake 30 minutes until tender.

Meanwhile, heat a nonstick skillet over medium heat. Add the chicken and cook 3 to 4 minutes, stirring, until browned and cooked through. Transfer the squash to a blender and blend until smooth. Finely chop the chicken, then add it to the squash.

Tip the mixture into a bowl, add the flour and parmesan, season with salt and pepper and bring the ingredients together until well blended. Turn onto a lightly floured surface and roll into a rope shape about ¾ inches in diameter. Cut into ¾-inch pieces using a sharp knife.

Bring a large pot of lightly salted water to a boil over high heat. Add about 10 gnocchi and boil 2 minutes just until they float to the surface. Lift out with a slotted spoon and set aside to drain while you cook the remaining gnocchi.

Melt a little of the butter in a small pan over medium heat. Add the mushrooms and fry about 5 minutes until soft. Season with salt and pepper to taste. Meanwhile, heat the remaining butter in a skillet over medium-high heat. Add the gnocchi and sage and toss in the butter for a few minutes until golden.

Serve the gnocchi hot, right from the pan, with the fried mushrooms and wilted greens.

Serves 4
Preparation time: 30 minutes
Cooking time: 45 minutes

14 ounces butternut squash, peeled, cut in half and seeded
1 tablespoon olive oil
12 ounces chicken, cut into small pieces
heaped ½ cup pasta flour, plus extra for dusting
2 tablespoons shredded parmesan cheese
¼ cup unsalted butter
2 tablespoons chopped sage leaves
3 cups button mushrooms
sea salt and freshly ground black pepper
1 recipe quantity Wilted Greens (see page 217), to serve

Chicken, chorizo & lima bean stew

This is really quick to put together, then you can just leave it in the oven to cook slowly until all the flavors have married perfectly. When I first made the dish on a British television morning show, I planned to use pork belly , but we had to make a last-minute substitution because another chef had made a pork belly dish the day before, so we replaced the pork with chicken. It was one of those moments when you change an element of a recipe, for instance, because you've run out of that ingredient, and you end up getting something even better than the original.

Heat the oven to 315°F. Heat half the oil in a stovetop ovenproof dish over medium heat. Add the chicken and cook a few minutes, stirring, until lightly colored on all sides. Remove the chicken from the dish and set aside. Add the remaining oil to the pan with the onion, garlic and bacon, and fry 3 to 4 minutes. Stir in the smoked paprika and chorizo, and cook 3 minutes longer until blended.

Add the red wine, tomatoes and tomato paste, return the chicken to the dish, then pour in enough water to just cover the ingredients. Cover the pot with a lid or aluminum foil, place in the oven and bake 1½ hours.

Stir in the lima beans, then cover and return the pot to the oven for 20 minutes longer until the butter beans have soaked up the juices and are heated through.

Remove from the oven and stir in the chopped spinach and half the cilantro. Season with salt and pepper to taste, then gently stir together. Sprinkle with the remaining cilantro and serve with steamed rice, or chunks of fresh bread and butter.

Serves 4
Preparation time: 15 minutes
Cooking time: 2 hours

2 tablespoons olive oil
1 pound 2 ounces skinless boneless
   chicken thighs, cut into chunks
1 onion, finely chopped
2 garlic cloves, crushed
⅔ cup smoked bacon or pancetta,
   cut into pieces
1 teaspoon smoked paprika
½ chorizo, roughly cubed
scant ½ cup red wine
1 x 15-ounce can tomato puree
1 tablespoon tomato paste
1½ cups drained canned lima beans
1¾ cups spinach leaves, roughly chopped
2 tablespoons roughly chopped cilantro
   leaves
sea salt and freshly ground black pepper
steamed rice, or chunks of bread and
   butter, to serve

Classic coq au vin

This classic chicken recipe has a great combination of flavors that makes for a lovely, rich, hearty stew—great to serve at any time of the year, but especially good on a cold winter's day. This is a particular favorite since I remember my mom making it when we were growing up.

Heat the oven to 350°F. Season the chicken with salt and pepper, then dust in the flour. Heat the oil in an ovenproof skillet or flameproof Dutch oven over high heat. Add the chicken and fry about 10 minutes until lightly browned on all sides. Remove from the pan and set aside.

Turn the heat down to medium and add the butter. Add the onion and garlic and fry 2 minutes. Add the bacon, mushrooms and shallots, and fry 3 to 4 minutes, then remove from the pan and add to the chicken.

Turn the heat up again, add the wine and deglaze the pan by stirring to remove any caramelized bits stuck to the bottom of the pan. Boil 2 minutes until the wine has reduced by half, then add the broth and bring to a boil.

Return the chicken and bacon mixture to the pan, cover with a lid, place in the oven and bake 35 to 40 minutes until the juices from the chicken run clear when the thickest part of the thigh is pierced with the tip of a sharp knife. Serve on its own or with boiled new potatoes.

Serves 4
Preparation time: 20 minutes, plus making the broth
Cooking time: 1 hour

4 chicken drumsticks, skin on
4 chicken thighs, skin on
scant ⅓ cup all-purpose flour
2 tablespoons olive oil
2 tablespoons unsalted butter
1 onion, finely chopped
1 garlic clove, chopped
2 thick strips smoked Canadian bacon, rind removed, finely chopped
2 ounces crimini mushrooms, quartered
14 small round shallots or pearl onions
⅔ cup red wine
generous 2 cups Chicken Broth (see page 197)
sea salt and freshly ground black pepper
boiled new potatoes with butter and parsley, to serve

Chicken stroganoff with saffron-braised rice

Stroganoff was one of the first dishes I put on the menu when I first started cooking so it's a real nostalgia trip for me. To soak up all that lovely creamy sauce, my first choice is always to serve it with saffron rice, although you might prefer some freshly boiled plain rice.

Heat the oven to 400°F. Melt the butter in a pan over medium heat, add the onion and garlic and cook 1 minute, stirring. Add the chicken strips and cook 2 to 3 minutes on each side, then remove everything from the pan.

Return the pan to a high heat, add the brandy and deglaze the pan by stirring to remove any caramelized bits stuck to the bottom. Add the broth, bring to a boil and boil 2 minutes until reduced to one-third. Stir in the cream, then the smoked paprika and cayenne.

Return the chicken and onion mixture to the pan and simmer 5 minutes, stirring occasionally. Season with salt and pepper to taste, then add the parsley.

Meanwhile, melt the butter for the rice in a stovetop and ovenproof dish over medium heat. Add the shallots and cook 2 to 3 minutes. Add the rice and cook 1 minute, then add the broth and saffron, season with a little salt and pepper and bring to a boil. Cover with a lid and bake 15 minutes until the rice is tender and the liquid is absorbed.

Stir the rice and season with salt and pepper to taste. Serve with the creamy stroganoff.

Serves 4
Preparation time: 20 minutes,
  plus making the broth
Cooking time: 20 minutes

2 tablespoons unsalted butter
1 onion, finely chopped
1 garlic clove, finely chopped
4 skinless chicken breasts, cut into strips
3 tablespoons brandy
½ cup Chicken Broth (see page 197)
⅓ cup heavy cream
1 teaspoon smoked paprika
¼ teaspoon cayenne pepper
1 tablespoon chopped parsley leaves
sea salt and freshly ground black pepper

FOR THE SAFFRON-BRAISED RICE
3½ tablespoons unsalted butter
3 small shallots, finely chopped
1⅔ cups long-grain rice
generous 2½ cups Chicken or Vegetable
  Broth (see page 197)
1 tablespoon saffron strands

Thai green chicken & spinach curry with sag aloo

I'm a big fan of Thai spices like lemongrass and lime leaf—as you may have guessed if you have been trying out my recipes. They strike a lovely balance of freshness and flavor, with that spicy heat that rounds off the dish. Pairing it with an Indian dish may seem unlikely but it works.

Heat the oil in a large skillet or wok over medium-high heat. Add the curry paste and cook 3 to 4 minutes, stirring. Add the chicken and cook 3 minutes, then add the coconut milk and broth. Bring to a boil, then turn the heat down to low and simmer 10 to 15 minutes until the chicken is cooked through. Add the green beans and cook 3 to 4 minutes longer.

Meanwhile, to make the sag aloo, heat the oil in a skillet over medium heat. Add the onion and spices and cook 3 to 4 minutes until softened and well blended. Add the potatoes and stir to coat in the spices, then add the baby spinach and cook 1 to 2 minutes until softened.

Stir the spinach into the curry and serve with the sag aloo and some sticky rice.

Serves 4
Preparation time: 20 minutes, plus making the curry paste and broth
Cooking time: 30 minutes

2 tablespoons olive oil
1 recipe quantity Thai Curry Paste (see page 205)
1¼ pounds skinless boneless chicken thighs, cut into about ¾-inch pieces
1¼ cups coconut milk
1¾ cups Chicken Broth (see page 197)
4 ounces trimmed green beans
1 cup spinach leaves, roughly chopped
cooked short-grain rice, to serve

FOR THE SAG ALOO
2 tablespoons olive oil
1 onion, thinly sliced
2 teaspoons ground cumin
1 teaspoon ground coriander
1 teaspoon turmeric
2 teaspoons garam masala
3 cups cooked potatoes, cut into chunks
2 cups baby spinach leaves, roughly chopped

Kofta chicken & cashew curry

This is a beautifully mild, creamy curry sauce but still has plenty of flavor, with the smooth, rich taste of the cashews and chicken absorbing the warm spices. I like to serve it with saffron rice but plain boiled rice is good, too. And perhaps add a few pappadams and some mango chutney.

Mix together all the kofta ingredients, season with salt and pepper, cover and chill 30 minutes in the refrigerator.

Meanwhile, toast the cashews in a dry pan over medium heat 3 minutes, tossing frequently, until lightly browned. Tip out of the pan onto a plate. Put half the cashews into a spice grinder or small food processor along with the garlic, ginger, chili and onion and 2 to 3 tablespoons water, and blitz to a smooth paste. Set aside.

Remove the kofta mixture from the refrigerator and roll into walnut-size balls. Heat half the clarified butter in a large skillet over medium heat. Add the koftas and fry 4 to 5 minutes until cooked through and nicely browned on all sides. Remove from the pan and keep them warm.

Wipe out the pan, then return it to medium heat and melt the remaining clarified butter. Add the cashew and onion paste and cook 3 minutes, stirring, until fragrant. Add the cumin, ground coriander and curry powder, and cook 1 to 2 minutes, stirring. Stir in 1 cup water and add the bay leaf and cinnamon stick and a large pinch of salt and pepper. Bring to a boil, then turn the heat down to low and simmer 2 to 3 minutes until the sauce has thickened and reduced slightly. Stir in the cream and cardamom.

Spoon a mound of saffron rice on each serving plate and top with the koftas. Spoon some of the sauce over them and put the rest in a gravy boat to serve separately. Sprinkle with the cilantro leaves and the remaining cashews and serve with a spoonful of mango chutney.

Serves 4
Preparation time: 15 minutes, plus 30 minutes chilling, and making the butter
Cooking time: 20 minutes

FOR THE KOFTAS
1¾ cups ground chicken
¾-inch piece ginger root, peeled and finely chopped
1 teaspoon turmeric
2 teaspoons garam masala
2 garlic cloves, finely chopped
2 tablespoons chopped cilantro leaves
2 tablespoons chopped mint leaves
sea salt and freshly ground black pepper

FOR THE KOFTA CURRY SAUCE
2 tablespoons whole cashews
2 garlic cloves
½-inch piece ginger root, peeled and finely chopped
½ green chili, seeded
1 small onion, quartered
2 tablespoons Clarified Butter (see page 196)
1 teaspoon ground cumin
1 teaspoon ground coriander
½ teaspoon Madras curry powder
1 bay leaf
½ cinnamon stick
⅓ cup heavy cream
½ teaspoon ground cardamom

1 recipe quantity Saffron Rice (see page 210)
1 tablespoon cilantro leaves
Mango Chutney (see page 206), to serve

Moroccan chicken & chickpea tagine

North African-style recipes often feature sweet and savory combinations, as does this Moroccan-inspired dish. If you don't have a Moroccan tagine—the distinctive conical Middle Eastern cooking pot—use any stovetop Dutch oven or cast-iron pan with a tight-fitting lid.

Heat the oil in a tagine or stovetop Dutch oven. Add the chicken and fry until just colored on all sides, then remove from the dish, using a slotted spoon.

Add the onions and garlic to the dish and fry 3 minutes until softened, then stir in the spices and fry 1 to 2 minutes until well blended. Stir in the soaked chickpeas, the raisins, tomatoes and lime leaf, and return the chicken to the dish.

Cover and simmer about 1 hour until the meat is tender and the sauce is thick. (Alternatively, cook in a heated oven at 350°F for the same length of time.)

When the tagine is almost ready, put the couscous in a heatproof bowl. Bring the broth to a boil in a pan over high heat, then pour it over the couscous and stir well. Cover with plastic wrap and let stand 10 minutes until soft. Drain off any excess liquid.

Serve the chicken right from the pot on generous piles of couscous.

Serves 4
Preparation time: 15 minutes, plus overnight soaking, and making the broth
Cooking time: 1¼ hours

2 tablespoons olive oil

2 skinless chicken breasts, cut into chunks

4 skinless boneless chicken thighs, cut into chunks

2 onions, thinly sliced

2 garlic cloves, finely chopped

1 tablespoon smoked paprika

1½ teaspoons ground cumin

1 teaspoon turmeric

1 teaspoon peeled and grated ginger root

scant 1 cup dried chickpeas, soaked overnight, then drained

¾ cup raisins

1 x 15-ounce can crushed tomatoes

1 kaffir lime leaf

1½ cups couscous

1¼ cups Vegetable Broth (see page 197)

Chili chocolate chicken

This dish is full of flavor but not over-spicy, although if do you like your food hot, then you could add some chopped chili or increase the amount of chili powder in your version. Never be afraid to experiment and personalize recipes so they are exactly how you like them. Chili and chocolate is a very ancient combination and well worth a try.

Heat the oil and butter in a large pan over medium heat. Add the onion, garlic and red pepper, and cook 3 to 4 minutes until softened. Add the chicken and cook with the vegetables, stirring to break up the ground meat, about 6 minutes until the chicken is lightly colored.

Mix in the smoked paprika, chili powder, tomatoes, kidney beans, broth and sugar, then bring to a boil, turn the heat down to low, partially cover with a lid, and simmer 45 to 60 minutes until the juices run clear when the thickest part of the chicken is pierced with the tip of a sharp knife and the sauce is thick. Season with salt and pepper to taste.

Spoon the chili into bowls, then drop a piece of chocolate into each bowl and leave it to melt over the top. Serve with freshly baked bread.

Serves 4
Preparation time: 20 minutes,
 plus making the broth
Cooking time: 1 hour 10 minutes

1 tablespoon olive oil
1 tablespoon unsalted butter
1 large onion, finely chopped
2 garlic cloves, finely chopped
1 red bell pepper, seeded and finely
 chopped
2¼ cups ground chicken
1 teaspoon smoked paprika
1 teaspoon chili powder
1 x 15-ounce can crushed tomatoes
1 x 15-ounce can red kidney beans,
 drained
⅔ cup Chicken Broth (see page 197)
1 tablespoon dark brown sugar
4 ounces dark chocolate, 70% cocoa
 solids, broken into 4 pieces
sea salt and freshly ground black pepper
crusty bread, to serve

Chicken in a pot

It is said that this dish was originally created by King Henry IV of England so it has a royal pedigree. With lots of fresh vegetables, a light broth and beautifully juicy chicken, this 21st-century version is equally regal.

Bring the broth to a boil in a large soup pot over high heat. Add all the vegetables and herbs for the broth. Put the whole chicken in the soup pot, reduce the heat to low, cover with a lid and simmer 50 minutes until the juices run clear when the thickest part of the chicken is pierced with the tip of a sharp knife.

Carefully lift out the chicken, then strain the broth, discard the broth vegetables and return the strained broth to the pot over medium heat. Put the chicken back in the pot, add the prepared vegetables and season with salt and pepper to taste. Return to a boil, then turn the heat down to low, cover with a lid and simmer 20 to 30 minutes longer until the vegetables are tender.

Lift out the chicken and carve it into portions. Serve with some of the vegetables and potatoes. Spoon a little of the broth over the top and sprinkle with the parsley and tarragon.

Serves 4 to 6
Preparation time: 15 minutes, plus making the broth
Cooking time: 1½ hours

FOR THE CHICKEN & VEGETABLE BROTH

4⅓ cups Chicken Broth (see page 197)
1 garlic bulb, cut in half horizontally
2 carrots, peeled and cut in half
2 celery stalks, cut into chunks
1 onion, quartered
2 leeks, trimmed and cut in half
1 bay leaf
1 bunch of parsley
2 thyme sprigs
10 black peppercorns
1 lemon verbena sprig

FOR THE CHICKEN

1 large chicken, about 5½ pounds
4 carrots, peeled and cut into sticks
3 leeks, trimmed and cut into chunks
2 small fennel bulbs, trimmed and cut into quarters
14 ounces small new potatoes
2 tablespoons chopped parsley leaves
1 tablespoon chopped tarragon leaves
sea salt and freshly ground black pepper

Homemade chicken & pancetta sausages with mustard mashed potatoes

Don't be put off by thinking it's difficult to make your own sausages—all you need are some sausage casings, which you can buy from your butcher or online. Your first attempts might be a bit lumpy but if you follow this recipe, they'll taste great.

Mix together the ground chicken, pancetta, thyme, nutmeg, sugar, salt and pepper in a bowl, cover with plastic wrap and chill at least 2 hours in the refrigerator.

If you have a sausage maker, use it to fill the skins with the meat mixture until you've used all the meat. If you don't have a sausage maker, spoon the mixture into a pastry bag with a large plain tip and pipe the mixture into the sausage skins, twisting the skins to form the end of each sausage and the start of the next, to give you 8 individual sausages. Cut into individual sausages.

Heat the oil in a large skillet over medium-high heat. Add the sausages and fry about 15 minutes, turning frequently, until browned and cooked through.

Meanwhile, bring a large pot of lightly salted water to a boil over high heat. Add the potatoes, return to a boil, then turn down the heat and simmer about 10 minutes until tender. Drain, then let air dry for a couple of minutes. Put them back in the pan, add the butter and mash until smooth, then mash in the mustard and cream and season with salt and pepper to taste.

Serve the sausages with the buttery mustard mashed potatoes and a drizzle of red wine sauce.

Serves 4
Preparation time: 30 minutes,
  plus at least 2 hours chilling
Cooking time: 15 minutes

1¾ pounds coarsely ground chicken,
  preferably thigh and breast meat
10 slices of pancetta, finely chopped
1 tablespoon finely chopped thyme leaves
1 teaspoon grated nutmeg
1½ teaspoons sugar
1 tablespoon sea salt
1 tablespoon freshly ground black pepper
3 tablespoons olive oil
1 recipe quantity Red Wine Sauce (see
  page 198), to serve

FOR THE MUSTARD MASHED POTATOES
1½ pounds baking potatoes, peeled and
  cut into small pieces
3 tablespoons unsalted butter
2 tablespoons wholegrain mustard
¼ cup heavy cream
sea salt and freshly ground black pepper

Confit chicken with herb pearl barley

To confit chicken is basically slow cooking it in duck or goose fat or oil, and is a preserving method used for fish, meat—especially duck—and also some vegetables. The cooked meat becomes so tender that it just falls off the bone and it can be kept, covered in the fat or oil, in an airtight container in the refrigerator for up to a couple of weeks.

Heat the oven to 200°F. Heat the sunflower oil in a large, deep stovetop and ovenproof pot over medium heat and add the juniper berries, peppercorns, cardamom, mustard seeds and 2 of the star anise. Bring to 180°F, so just below a boil. Carefully add the chicken legs so they are just covered in the oil. Cover with a lid, transfer to the oven and cook 2½ hours. Insert a knife into the flesh. If it slips through to the bone, the legs are done. If not, return them to the oven for 30 minutes longer.

Carefully remove the chicken legs from the oil, taking care they don't fall apart, and drain 5 minutes on paper towels. Cover the legs with plastic wrap and chill up to 2 days in the refrigerator, or until needed.

Meanwhile, rinse the pearl barley under cold running water, then drain and put in a pan with 1 cup of the broth, the bay leaves and remaining star anise. Bring to a boil over high heat, then turn the heat down to very low and simmer 20 to 25 minutes until cooked, stirring every 5 minutes. Remove from the heat.

Heat or turn the oven up to 400°F. Put the confit chicken legs in a roasting pan, drizzle with a little of the olive oil and season with salt and pepper. Roast 10 to 15 minutes until the chicken is golden and the skin crisp.

Heat the oil and butter in a large skillet over medium heat. Add the shallots and garlic, then the chopped vegetables and sauté for 3 minutes. Stir in the herbs and the cooked pearl barley along with the remaining broth. Season with salt and pepper and bring to a boil, then simmer 5 to 8 minutes until the vegetables are tender. Top the pearl barley with the chicken legs and serve with wilted greens.

Serves 4
Preparation time: 25 minutes, plus chilling (optional), and making the broth
Cooking time: 3 hours

3 quarts sunflower oil
8 juniper berries
12 black peppercorns
2 black cardamom pods
4 teaspoons mustard seeds
4 star anise
4 chicken legs, skin on
½ cup pearl barley
2½ cups Chicken Broth (see page 197)
2 bay leaves
2 tablespoons olive oil
2 tablespoons unsalted butter
2 shallots, sliced
4 garlic cloves, crushed
½ celery root, peeled and finely chopped
2 parsnips, peeled and finely chopped
2 carrots, peeled and finely chopped
leaves from 2 thyme sprigs, chopped
leaves from 2 rosemary sprigs, chopped
4 teaspoons chopped chives
sea salt and freshly ground black pepper
1 recipe quantity Wilted Greens (see page 217), to serve

Yakitori chicken with apricot bulgur

Here I have combined flavors from two continents—the Japanese flavors of mirin, sake and soy, with the Middle Eastern sweet fruits and grains. I love the fact that contemporary cooking has broken down so many barriers to experimenting with new ideas.

Put the bulgur in a large heatproof bowl, then pour the hot broth over it and let stand 25 to 30 minutes. Soak some wooden skewers in cold water.

Meanwhile, put the marinade ingredients in a pot over medium heat and warm gently until the sugar is dissolved, stirring occasionally. Pour into a bowl or measuring jug, let cool slightly, then chill 15 minutes in the refrigerator.

Put the chicken pieces into a bag or bowl and pour the cooled yakitori marinade over them. Cover and let marinate about 30 minutes in the refrigerator.

Heat a ridged grill pan or barbecue until hot. Thread about 4 pieces of chicken onto each skewer.

Drain any excess liquid from the bulgur, then stir in the lemon zest and juice. Mix in the honey and chives, then the red onion and apricots. Season with salt and pepper to taste, then set aside.

Cook the skewers 1 to 2 minutes on each side until cooked through and tender. Let rest 1 minute, then serve with the apricot bulgur.

Serves 4
Preparation time: 15 minutes,
   plus 1 hour soaking and marinating,
   and making the broth
Cooking time: 10 minutes

8 skinless boneless chicken thighs,
   cut into ¾-inch cubes

FOR THE APRICOT BULGUR
⅔ cup bulgur
2½ cups Chicken Broth (see page 197),
   boiling
grated zest and juice of ½ lemon
1 tablespoon honey
2 tablespoons chopped chives
1 red onion, thinly sliced
1⅓ cups ready-to-eat dried apricots,
   finely chopped
sea salt and freshly ground black pepper

FOR THE YAKITORI MARINADE
1 cup soy sauce
½ cup Chicken Broth (see page 197)
½ cup sake
½ cup mirin
¼ cup dark brown sugar

Teriyaki-glazed chicken breasts with sesame greens

Teriyaki is a traditional cooking method used in Japanese cuisine, consisting of cooking a piece of meat or fish using a sweet marinade, usually containing soy, mirin or sake, sugar and sometimes honey. When cooking, you should try to baste the meat at least once to give you a rich, sweet glaze. I've added a little garlic, ginger and Worcestershire sauce to give it extra flavor.

Whisk together all the marinade ingredients in a nonmetallic bowl. Add the chicken breasts and turn to coat in the marinade, then cover with plastic wrap and let marinate at least 1 hour in the refrigerator.

Heat the oven to 350°F. Heat the olive oil in a skillet over medium heat. Lift the chicken out of the marinade, add to the pan and fry a few minutes on each side until browned.

Transfer to a roasting pan, brush with some of the remaining marinade and roast 12 to 15 minutes until the juices run clear when the thickest part of the chicken is pierced with the tip of a sharp knife. Cover with aluminum foil and let rest in a warm place while you cook the greens.

To cook the sesame greens, heat the sesame oil in a heavy skillet or wok over medium heat. Add the sliced leeks, then the sugar snap peas and finally the zucchini, and fry 3 to 4 minutes, tossing together gently. Add the soy sauce and sesame seeds, season with salt and pepper, and cook for 1 minute longer.

Serve the chicken and greens hot with some creamy mashed potatoes.

Serves 4
Preparation time: 15 minutes,
  plus at least 1 hour marinating
Cooking time: 25 minutes

4 skinless chicken breasts
1 tablespoon olive oil
1 recipe quantity Creamy Mashed Potatoes
  (see page 212), to serve

FOR THE SESAME GREENS

2 tablespoons sesame oil
2 leeks, trimmed and thinly sliced
5 ounces sugar snap peas
2 zucchini, cubed
2 tablespoons light soy sauce
¼ cup sesame seeds
sea salt and freshly ground black pepper

FOR THE TERIYAKI MARINADE

2 cups soy sauce
½ cup mirin or sake
¼ cup dark brown sugar
2 garlic cloves, grated
1 teaspoon peeled and grated ginger root
1 teaspoon Worcestershire sauce

Crisp-skinned chicken with sweet potato puree, kale & crisp leeks

Great at anytime of the year, but I think real comfort food like this is ideal for those cold winter evenings. With the delicious crisp skin on succulent chicken, seasonal buttered kale and lovely crisp leeks on top, it'll banish those winter chills.

To make the sweet potato puree, bring a large pot of lightly salted water to a boil over high heat. Add the sweet potatoes and boil 10 to 15 minutes until tender. Drain, then transfer to a blender and blitz to a puree. Gradually blend in three-quarters of the butter, then the cream, and season with salt and pepper to taste. Spoon into a pot, cover and set aside.

Heat the oven to 350°F. Season the chicken with a little salt and pepper on both sides. Heat the oil in a large ovenproof skillet, add the chicken, skin-side down, and fry 2 to 3 minutes until golden. Turn the chicken over and cook 2 to 3 minutes longer. Turn back onto the skin side and put the pan in the oven 10 to 15 minutes until the juices run clear when the thickest part of the chicken is pierced with the tip of a sharp knife.

Meanwhile, make the crisp leeks. Pour 1¼ inches oil into a pot over medium heat until the oil reaches 350°F, when a cube of bread browns in 60 seconds. Season the flour with salt and pepper, then dust the leek strips in the seasoned flour. Lower about one-quarter of the leek strips into the hot oil and fry about 2 minutes until crisp, then drain on paper towels. Keep it warm while you fry the rest.

To cook the kale, melt the remaining butter in a skillet over high heat. Add the kale and 3 tablespoons water and stir to steam the kale until softened. Turn the heat down and season with salt and pepper.

Warm through the sweet potato puree over low heat. Remove the chicken from the oven, let rest for a minute, then slice on the diagonal. Serve with the sweet potato puree and kale.

Serves 4
Preparation time: 30 minutes
Cooking time: 35 minutes

2 large sweet potatoes, peeled and cut into small chunks
3½ cups cubed unsalted butter
3 tablespoons heavy cream
4 statler breasts or large chicken breasts, skin on
1 tablespoon olive oil, plus extra for frying the leek
¾ cup self-rising flour
1 large leek, trimmed and thinly sliced into strips
9 ounces kale, stalks removed
sea salt and freshly ground black pepper

Portuguese chicken with roasted garlic & pine nut & spinach

We used to spend our vacations at my grandparents' timeshare in Portugal, and everywhere you went they served the classic Portuguese piri piri chicken. So here's a simple dish to remind you of sun-drenched summer vacations.

Put all the marinade ingredients into a blender and blitz to a puree. Put the chicken breasts into a nonmetallic bowl, cover with the marinade and rub it into the meat. Cover with plastic wrap and marinate 1 hour in the refrigerator.

Heat the oven to 350°F. Toast the pine nuts in a dry pot over medium heat for a few minutes, shaking the pan continuously, until they start to brown. Tip out of the hot pan and set aside.

Heat the oil in an ovenproof skillet over medium heat. Add the chicken breasts and fry 2 minutes on each side. Transfer the pan to the oven and roast 10 minutes until the chicken is cooked through and the juices run clear when the thickest part of the chicken is pierced with the tip of a sharp knife. Let rest while you cook the spinach.

Heat the butter in a pot over medium heat, add the spinach and keep turning until the spinach starts to wilt. Add the toasted pine nuts, squeeze the roasted garlic cloves out of their skins into the pan and stir the spinach 1 to 2 minutes until warmed through and mixed together but still retaining the bright green color. Season with salt and pepper and serve with the chicken. Serve with a few fresh baby spinach leaves.

Serves 4
Preparation time: 15 minutes, plus 1 hour marinating, and making the roasted garlic
Cooking time: 20 minutes

4 skinless chicken breasts
1/3 cup pine nuts
1 tablespoon olive oil
2 tablespoons unsalted butter
3 1/2 cups spinach leaves
1 recipe quantity Roasted Garlic (see page 204)
sea salt and freshly ground black pepper
a few baby spinach leaves, to serve

FOR THE PORTUGUESE MARINADE
1 red onion, quartered
3 garlic cloves
1 red chili with seeds
1 tablespoon smoked paprika
1 teaspoon chopped thyme leaves
grated zest and juice of 1/2 lemon
1/2 red bell pepper, seeded
1 tablespoon olive oil
1 teaspoon salt

Roast chicken with mushroom & leek lentils

One of the reasons I love cooking is the vast range of interesting ingredients available. I'm a big fan of grains and legumes but sometimes they can be rather bland, so this is a great recipe to really show your guests that eating healthy grains and legumes isn't boring as long as you add lots of flavor during cooking.

Heat the oven to 400°F. Bring the broth to a boil in a large pot over medium heat, then turn the heat down to low and let simmer.

Melt half the butter in a large skillet over medium heat. Add the onion and garlic and cook 3 minutes until softened. Stir in the lentils and the wine until absorbed.

Start to add 2½ cups of the hot broth, a ladleful at a time, and cook, stirring continuously until the liquid is absorbed before adding more. Repeat this process until all the broth is absorbed. This should take about 20 minutes. Cook the lentils for 10 minutes longer until they are just dry and gently caramelizing, stirring to prevent them sticking to the base of the pan. Transfer to a bowl and set aside.

Season the chicken with salt and pepper on both sides. Heat the oil in a large stovetop and ovenproof dish over medium heat. Add the chicken breasts, skin-side down first, and cook 2 to 3 minutes on each side until just browned. Transfer the pan to the oven and roast 20 minutes until the juices run clear when the thickest part of the chicken is pierced with a sharp knife.

Meanwhile, return the pan in which the lentils were cooked to a medium heat, add the remaining butter, the mushrooms and leeks and cook 4 minutes until softened. Return the lentils to the pan and stir together well. Add half the remaining broth and stir until it is all absorbed, then add the remaining broth, the soy sauce, Worcestershire sauce, chives and thyme, and cook about 10 minutes until the lentils have a loose consistency like a risotto so it just holds its shape. Sit the chicken on top of the lentils, sprinkle with some parsnip crisps or crisp shallots, and serve with wilted greens.

Serves 4
Preparation time: 20 minutes, plus making the broth
Cooking time: 45 minutes

3½ cups Chicken Broth (see page 197)
2 tablespoons unsalted butter
½ onion, finely chopped
1 garlic clove, finely chopped
1 cup French lentils, rinsed and drained
3 tablespoons white wine
4 chicken breasts, skin on
2 tablespoons olive oil
1¾ cups mixed field mushrooms or wild mushrooms, thinly sliced
1⅔ cups trimmed and thinly sliced leeks
2 tablespoons light soy sauce
2 teaspoons Worcestershire sauce
2 tablespoons chopped chives
1 teaspoon chopped thyme leaves
sea salt and freshly ground black pepper
1 recipe quantity Parsnip Crisps (see page 215) or Crisp Fried Shallots (see page 205), to serve
1 recipe quantity Wilted Greens (see page 217), to serve

Lemon verbena & thyme-roasted chicken

Brining a chicken is a great way to keep the meat moist when you are roasting, as well as adding flavor to the meat. For my recipe, I'm using lemon verbena, but you can use lemon thyme instead. Either way, while it is cooking, the herbs make a pretty impressive aroma that everyone will appreciate. The number of servings obviously depends on the size of bird, but you can use the same principles and adjust the quantities for smaller or a larger bird.

You will need a pot large enough to hold both chicken and brine and fit in the refrigerator. Put 6 quarts water in the pot, add the brine ingredients and stir to dissolve the salt. Add the chicken, making sure it is covered in brine. Cover and marinate about 12 hours or overnight in the refrigerator.

Heat the oven to 315°F. Remove the chicken from the brine and shake off any excess liquid. Stand it on a clean cloth for a few minutes to drain, then pat the chicken dry. Pour the oil over the chicken and rub it into the skin, then season with salt and pepper.

Strain the vegetables and herbs out of the brine and put the vegetables in a flameproof roasting pan. Put the herbs inside the chicken, then put the chicken on top of the vegetables. (I don't truss the chicken, so it cooks evenly throughout.) Roast 1½ hours, then turn the heat up to 400°F and roast 15 to 20 minutes longer to get the skin crisp. The inside of the chicken closest to the bone should reach 175°F on a meat thermometer. If you don't have a thermometer, the juices should run clear when the thickest part of the thigh is pierced with the tip of a sharp knife. If there is any red or pink, cook a little longer. Lift the chicken out of the pan, cover it and leave it in a warm place 5 to 10 minutes while you make the gravy.

Put the roasting pan with the vegetables and juices over medium heat. Add the red wine sauce and cook 3 to 4 minutes, deglazing the pan by stirring to remove any caramelized bits stuck to the bottom. Strain through a fine strainer, then serve with the roast chicken, roast potatoes and wilted greens.

Serves 8
Preparation time: 20 minutes, plus 12 hours brining, and making the sauce
Cooking time: 2 hours

1 recipe quantity Brine (see page 17)
1 large chicken, about 5½ pounds
2 tablespoons canola oil
1 recipe quantity Red Wine Sauce (see page 198)
sea salt and freshly ground black pepper
1 recipe quantity Roast Potatoes (see page 212), to serve
1 recipe quantity Wilted Greens (see page 217), to serve

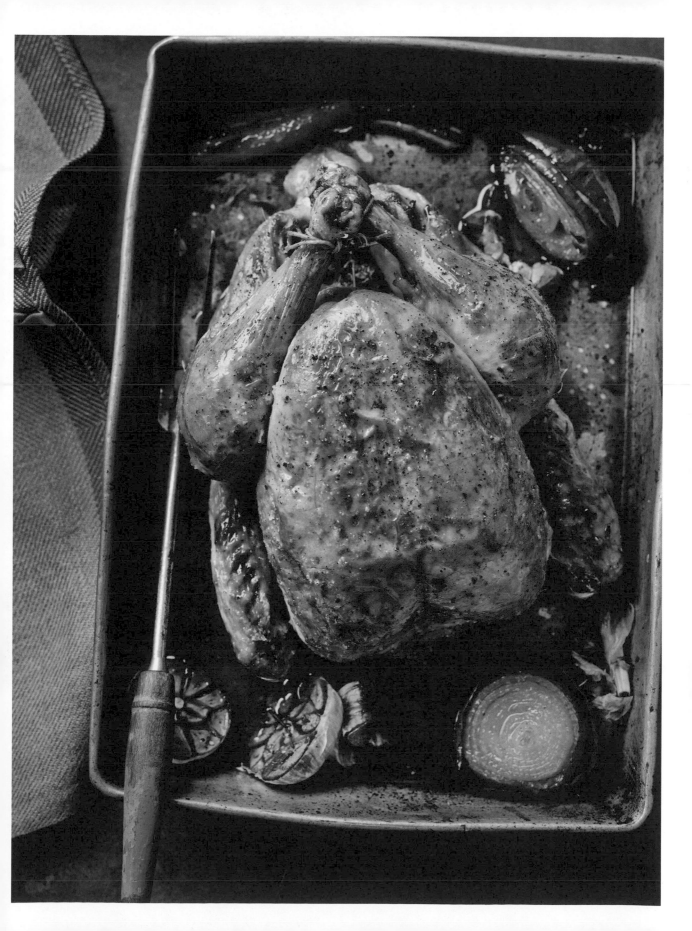

3

dinners & celebrations

Chicken & watercress soup with vegetable crisps

Making a soup was one of the first things I did when I started cooking, building up the flavors from the base with onions or shallots, and garlic sautéed in butter. If you want to become a good cook, start by making lots of soups and playing around with flavors and textures. This soup brings the peppery notes of watercress to the succulent chicken, with potato to thicken the soup and add both texture and flavor.

Melt the butter in a large pot over low heat. Turn the heat up to medium, add the chicken, onion, garlic and leek, and fry 2 to 3 minutes until soft.

Add the potato, broth and half the watercress, bring to a boil over medium heat, then turn the heat down to low and simmer about 20 minutes until the potatoes are tender and the juices run clear when the thickest part of the chicken is pierced with the tip of a sharp knife.

Remove the chicken from the soup and shred, using two forks. Blend the soup until smooth, using a blender or food processor, then add the remaining watercress and the spinach and blend again.

Return the soup and shredded chicken to the rinsed-out pan. Heat to a simmer, then cook 2 to 3 minutes until heated through. Drizzle with the cream, sprinkle with the thyme leaves and top with the sweet potato crisps. Serve with chunks of warm toast.

Serves 4
Preparation time: 15 minutes, plus making the broth and vegetable crisps
Cooking time: 30 minutes

3½ tablespoons unsalted butter
2 skinless chicken breasts, quartered
1 onion, thinly sliced
1 garlic clove, finely chopped
½ leek, trimmed and thinly sliced
1 large baking potato, peeled and cubed
4⅓ cups Vegetable Broth (see page 197)
2 cups watercress
2 cups spinach leaves, roughly chopped
2 tablespoons heavy cream
1 teaspoon chopped thyme leaves
1 recipe quantity Sweet Potato Crisps (see page 215)
toast or crusty bread, to serve

Chicken, wild mushroom & miso soup

This recipe uses dashi, which can be used not only as a soup broth but also as a dipping sauce or a sauce for rice and noodles. It is made with kombu—a dried seaweed—and dried bonito flakes. You should find the ingredients in the major supermarkets or in Asian markets.

Soak the kombu 30 minutes in cold water, then drain. Put in a pot, cover with 2 cups cold water and bring to a boil over high heat. Just before the water boils, remove the kombu using a slotted spoon. Add the bonito flakes and return to a boil. As soon as the water returns to a boil, remove from the heat and let stand about 10 minutes until the bonito flakes sink to the bottom, then let the broth stand for 5 minutes longer. Strain the broth into a clean pan and discard the bonito flakes and kombu. You should have 2 cups of the dashi broth.

Put the chicken, mushrooms, onion and carrots into the broth and bring to a boil over high heat. Turn the heat down to low and simmer 5 to 10 minutes until the vegetables are tender and the juices run clear which the thickest part of the chicken is pierced with the tip of a sharp knife. Add the spinach and tofu, if using, and simmer 2 minutes until the spinach is softened.

Put the miso paste in a small bowl, add a ladleful of the soup from the pan and stir until blended. Gently stir this back into the soup. Remove from the heat and add the scallions and the lime leaf. Serve with fresh bread or corn on the cob.

Serves 4
Preparation time: 20 minutes, plus 40 minutes soaking, and soaking the mushrooms
Cooking time: 20 minutes

FOR THE DASHI
4-inch piece of kombu
½ ounce dried bonito flakes

FOR THE SOUP
2 skinless chicken breasts, each cut into 8 pieces
4 dried wild mushrooms, soaked overnight, then strained and finely chopped
1 onion, thinly sliced
2 carrots, peeled and thinly sliced into matchsticks
1 cup baby spinach leaves
1½ cups cubed tofu (optional)
3 to 4 tablespoons miso paste
2 scallions, diagonally sliced
1 kaffir lime leaf, finely chopped
fresh bread or corn on the cob, to serve

Deconstructed crisp pancetta & charred-lettuce Caesar salad with anchovy straws

This is my modern version of a Caesar salad, with succulent chicken, crisp pancetta, a good cage-free eggs, crisp salad and a rich dressing. With its contemporary twist, this makes a special appetizer to serve to your friends—and tastes fantastic. You could also serve it as a perfect light lunch, so you can adapt the quantities to suit your guests' appetites.

Heat the oven to 350°F and line a cookie sheet with parchment paper. Put the pancetta on the prepared sheet, cover with another piece of parchment paper, then place a second cookie sheet on top. Bake 10 to 12 minutes until golden brown. Transfer to a wire rack to cool and crisp.

Meanwhile, season the chicken with salt and pepper. Heat the oil in a skillet over medium-high heat. Add the chicken, skin-side down, and fry 2 to 3 minutes on each side until golden. Transfer to a roasting pan and roast 15 minutes until the juices run clear when the thickest part of the chicken is pierced with the tip of a sharp knife. Cover and let rest in a warm place until ready to serve.

While the chicken is cooking, bring a pot of water to a boil over high heat. Gently lower the eggs into the water, then boil 6½ minutes. Lift the eggs out of the water, using a slotted spoon, put in a bowl of ice-cold water to stop them from cooking any more and let cool about 5 minutes. Peel in the water, to stop them from breaking, then drain and cut in half.

Heat a ridged grill pan over high heat. Add the lettuce, flat-side down, and cook 1 to 2 minutes on each side. This gives the lettuce a charred effect and a slightly smoky flavor, but keeps it nice and crunchy in the center.

Whisk together all the dressing ingredients in a nonmetallic bowl until blended, then pour into small shot glasses. Slice the chicken and put on top of the lettuce halves, top with the eggs, sprinkle with the crisp pancetta and serve with the dressing and anchovy straws.

Serves 4
Preparation time: 20 minutes, plus making the mayonnaise
Cooking time: 25 minutes

8 slices of pancetta
2 chicken breasts, skin on, sliced in half
1 teaspoon olive oil
4 cage-free eggs
2 heads of romaine lettuce, cut in half lengthwise
sea salt and freshly ground black pepper
1 recipe quantity Anchovy Straws (see page 209), to serve

FOR THE CAESAR DRESSING
1 teaspoon anchovy paste
2 tablespoons white wine vinegar
3 tablespoons Mayonnaise (see page 202)
2 tablespoons Dijon mustard
1 garlic clove, finely chopped
½ teaspoon lemon juice
⅔ cup olive oil
2 tablespoons shredded parmesan cheese

Chicken liver, orange, pea shoot & watercress salad

I used to hate chicken livers when I was growing up but over the years my palate has changed and now I love their soft texture. It is important to make sure you brown livers quickly but don't overcook them, otherwise they can go a bit dry. A touch of acidity helps to sharpen the flavor— I've used fresh orange segments to make this a great little salad for an appetizer or light lunch.

To make the croutons, heat the oven to 350°F. Cut the bread into long strips about ½- to ¾-inch thick, then cut across the strips to create cubes. Put on a baking sheet, drizzle with the oil, sprinkle with the thyme and rosemary, and season with the salt and pepper. Roast 8 to 10 minutes until golden and crisp. Remove from the oven and set aside.

Slice off the top and bottom of the oranges, then peel from top to bottom, using a small, sharp knife, to remove all the skin and the white pith, leaving you with the orange still in shape but without its skin. Holding the orange in one hand, you'll see the lines of the segments. Carefully slice lengthwise on the inside of one of the lines to the center then the same on the other side of the segment. The segment will just fall out. Repeat this with the whole of both oranges and set aside.

Put all the dressing ingredients in a bowl and whisk together until blended, then season with salt and pepper.

Heat the oil in a large skillet over high heat. Add the chicken livers and cook 2 to 3 minutes without moving or shaking the pan. Turn the livers over and cook 1 minute longer until the they are cooked but still slightly pink in the center (cut one open to check), then remove the pan from the heat and add the butter. Baste the livers with the melted butter. Remove the livers from the pan and let rest on a warm plate.

Mix together the watercress and pea shoots in a bowl, add the croutons, livers and orange segments, then drizzle over the dressing and toss together to serve.

Serves 4
Preparation time: 20 minutes
Cooking time: 15 minutes

2 large oranges
2 tablespoons olive oil
14 ounces chicken livers, trimmed (about 1¾ cups
1 tablespoon unsalted butter
⅔ cup watercress
⅔ cup pea shoots

FOR THE HERB CROUTONS
2 thick slices of day-old crusty bread
1 tablespoon olive oil
1 teaspoon chopped thyme leaves
1 teaspoon chopped rosemary leaves
1 teaspoon of sea salt
½ teaspoon crushed black peppercorns

FOR THE ORANGE DRESSING
2 tablespoons balsamic vinegar
juice of 1 orange, about ¼ cup
¼ cup olive oil
½ teaspoon Dijon mustard
sea salt and freshly ground black pepper

Tea-smoked chicken & miso-dressed salad

I'm a big fan of smoked chicken, and by using green tea in your smoking ingredients, you retain the soft texture of the chicken and give it a more subtle smokiness. Add the lovely fresh Swiss chard, heritage tomato and cucumber, and you get a super-light, fresh and summery salad with lots of color and a smoky, crunchy texture from the bacon. If you can't buy Swiss chard, use a selection of arugula, beet leaves and sorrel. If you prefer, you can replace the bacon with 2 tablespoons of mixed pumpkin seeds, sunflower seeds or toasted peanuts.

Use a large pot with a steamer attachment. Line the pot with a double layer of aluminum foil, then empty the contents of the tea bags in the center of the foil. Put the steamer on top and then the pot lid. Put the pot over a low to medium heat until you start to see the smoke rising into the steamer. Season the chicken breasts with salt and pepper, then put them in the steamer and cover with a lid. Let it smoke 30 to 40 minutes.

Meanwhile, if you are using the bacon, heat the broiler or a small skillet. Broil or sauté the bacon 5 minutes until crisp, turning occasionally, then chop.

Put the tomatoes, cucumber and Swiss chard in a bowl and toss together lightly. Sprinkle with the chopped bacon or the seeds or nuts.

Once the breasts are cooked, remove them from the steamer, cut into thin slices and add to the salad bowl. Sprinkle the miso dressing over them to serve.

Serves 4
Preparation time: 20 minutes, plus making the dressing
Cooking time: 40 minutes

FOR THE TEA-SMOKED CHICKEN
8 green-tea bags
4 skinless chicken breasts
sea salt and freshly ground black pepper

FOR THE TOMATO, SWISS CHARD & CUCUMBER SALAD
1 strip of thick-cut smoked bacon or 1 tablespoon pumpkin or sunflower seeds, or toasted peanuts
8 heritage tomatoes, sliced
1 cucumber, chopped
10 to 12 mixed Swiss chard leaves, roughly chopped
1 recipe quantity Miso Dressing (see page 203)

Chicken, mushroom & baby leek terrine

I like the extra flavor of crimini mushrooms, but you can use ordinary mushrooms instead if you don't have them. The terrine takes very little time to put together but makes an attractive and flavorful dish.

Bring a large pot of lightly salted water to a boil over high heat. Add the leeks and boil 2 minutes, then drain and put in a bowl of ice-cold water to stop them cooking any further, then drain again and put in a roasting pan.

Melt the butter in a skillet over low heat. Add the mushrooms and fry 2 to 3 minutes until just cooked but not losing their shape. Tip into the roasting pan along with the chicken, spinach, thyme and tarragon. Melt the duck fat, then pour it over the ingredients in the roasting pan and toss so they are coated in fat.

Line a 6¼- x 4½-inch terrine mold or loaf pan with plastic wrap, letting it overhang the edges. Using a spoon so there is a little fat in each layer, start layering the ingredients into the terrine: chicken, then mushrooms, leek and spinach, seasoning each layer with salt and pepper, then repeat until the terrine is full. Wrap the plastic wrap over the top, then press with a heavy weight, such as one or two full cans, and chill overnight in the refrigerator to set.

To serve, gently loosen the plastic wrap around the edges of the mold and turn the terrine out onto a cutting board. Cut into slices using a knife dipped in boiling water, then serve with spiced apple chutney and homemade bread.

Serves 8
Preparation time: 30 minutes, plus overnight chilling, and making the confit
Cooking time: 10 minutes

6 ounces baby leeks, trimmed
2 tablespoons unsalted butter
6 ounces crimini mushrooms, cut in half
3 confit skinless chicken breasts (see page 122), sliced into long strips
1 cup baby spinach leaves
1 teaspoon chopped thyme leaves
1 teaspoon tarragon leaves
scant 1 cup duck fat
sea salt and freshly ground black pepper
Spiced Apple Chutney (see page 206), to serve
homemade bread, to serve

Chicken, spinach, goat cheese & slow-roasted tomato terrine

This makes a perfect summer appetizer, especially as you can prepare it ahead of time and have everything ready before your guests arrive. If you have some leftover chicken from a roast, you could use that instead of cooking the chicken.

Put the broth, half the butter and the bay leaf in a pot over medium heat. Bring to a boil, then turn the heat down to low, add the chicken and simmer 10 to 15 minutes until the juices run clear when the thickest part of the chicken is pierced with the tip of a sharp knife. Drain and set aside, reserving the broth.

Line a 16¼- x 4½-inch terrine mold or loaf pan with plastic wrap, letting it overhang the edges. Melt the remaining butter in a pot over medium heat. Add the spinach and cook a few minutes, stirring, until just softened, then remove from the heat and set aside.

Warm the reserved broth in a pot over medium heat, then gently whisk in the gelatin.

Line the prepared mold with the prosciutto, letting it overhang the top enough to fold over and cover the top of the terrine. Start layering the ingredients into the terrine. Start with a layer of the chicken, then pour some of the broth over the top. Then make a layer of the tomatoes and moisten with broth. Next make a layer of the spinach and a little more broth, then finish with the crumbled goat cheese. Season with salt and pepper and scatter in the herbs. Wrap the prosciutto over the top. Wrap the plastic wrap over that, put a heavy weight on top, such as two full cans, and chill overnight in the refrigerator to set.

To serve, gently loosen the plastic wrap around the edges of the mold and turn the terrine out onto a cutting board. Cut into slices using a knife dipped in boiling water, then serve with freshly baked bread.

Serves 8
Preparation time: 40 minutes, plus overnight chilling, and making the broth and slow-roasted tomatoes
Cooking time: 25 minutes

1¼ cups Chicken Broth (see page 197)
2 tablespoons unsalted butter
1 bay leaf
3 skinless chicken breasts, each cut lengthwise into 4
7 cups spinach leaves
1 envelop gelatin
12 slices prosciutto
10 ounces Slow-Roasted Tomatoes (see page 218) or sun-ripened tomatoes
1 cup crumbled goat cheese
2 teaspoons chopped thyme leaves
2 teaspoons chopped chives
sea salt and freshly ground black pepper
fresh bread, to serve

Smoked chicken, mango & asparagus verrine

A verrine is a French dish in which the ingredients are layered in a small glass. I first discovered the verrine when I was doing some filming and was introduced to a lovely gentleman called Franc, who had written a book on them. I loved the visual aspect of it, with all the ingredients in one glass where the flavors marry together, and it works perfectly with smoked chicken and fresh asparagus in season to give you that lovely flavor of the countryside.

Bring a large pot of water to a boil over high heat. Add the asparagus, return to a boil and simmer 1 minute until just tender. Drain well, then put the asparagus into a bowl of ice-cold water to stop it from cooking any further.

Meanwhile, bring another pot of water to a boil over high heat. Gently lower the eggs into the water, then boil 6½ minutes. Lift the eggs out of the water, using a slotted spoon, put in a bowl of ice-cold water to stop them from cooking any more and let cool about 5 minutes. Peel in the water, to stop them from breaking, then drain and chop.

Mix together the chicken, mayonnaise, tarragon and chives and season with salt and pepper. Cut off the tips of the asparagus spears, cut them in half crosswise and set aside, then chop the rest of the stems into small pieces.

To assemble the verrine, have all your ingredients set out in front of you and have four wide, 10-ounce tumblers handy. Start with a layer of the chicken mixture at the bottom of each tumbler, then a layer of mango, then chopped asparagus, then tomato and egg, then finish with the asparagus tips. Chill until you are ready to serve.

Serves: 4
Preparation time: 20 minutes,
   plus making the mayonnaise
Cooking time: 10 minutes

12 asparagus spears
2 eggs
2 smoked skinless chicken breasts (see
   page 144), cut into ½- to ¾-inch pieces
2 tablespoons Mayonnaise (see page 202)
1 teaspoon chopped tarragon leaves
1 tablespoon chopped chives
1 ripe mango, peeled, pitted and chopped
3 vine tomatoes, seeded and chopped
sea salt and freshly ground black pepper

Confit chicken & charred pepper verrine

My second verrine uses the meltingly tender confit chicken—chicken legs cooked long and slow until they virtually fall apart. If you have some confit in the refrigerator, you can put this impressive appetizer together in no time.

Heat the broiler to high or use a gas flame to char the peppers over a naked flame for 3 to 4 minutes, turning until blistered and completely black. Put in a bowl, cover tightly with plastic wrap and set aside for 5 minutes. Scrape off the skins with your fingers, then cut the flesh into very thin strips.

Meanwhile, put the shredded chicken in a bowl, mix with the mayonnaise, season with salt and pepper to taste and set aside. Holding the ear of corn vertically on a cutting board, slice off the corn kernels, using a sharp knife, then discard the cobs.

To assemble the verrine, you will need four 10-ounce glasses, preferably slightly wider at the bottom. Spoon some chicken into the bottom of the glasses, then a layer of peppers, then some arugula, then cherry tomatoes. Repeat the process, making sure you vary the pieces so the verrines look as colorful and appetizing as possible. Sprinkle with crisp shallots and serve.

Serves 4
Preparation time: 20 minutes, plus making the confit and mayonnaise
Cooking time: 5 minutes

1 red bell pepper
1 green bell pepper
4 confit chicken legs (see page 122), shredded
3 tablespoons Mayonnaise (see page 202)
2 cooked ears of corn
1¾ cups arugula leaves
12 cherry tomatoes, cut in half
sea salt and freshly ground black pepper
1 recipe quantity Crisp Fried Shallots (see page 205), to serve

Zucchini, chicken & mozzarella tempura

Perfect for an impressive canapé or even just a simple snack, zucchini flowers have a lovely, delicate flavor and texture. The innovative twist in this recipe is created by stuffing them with a finely chopped chicken mixture, and dipping them in a tempura batter before deep-frying. You end up with a very light, crisp batter surrounding the tender chicken.

Put the chicken thighs in a pot and just cover with water. Bring to a boil over high heat, then turn the heat down to low and simmer 30 to 40 minutes until the juices run clear when the thickest part of the chicken is pierced with the tip of a sharp knife. Drain and let cool, then chop finely.

Mix together the chicken, arugula, mozzarella, cream cheese and chives, and season with salt and pepper. Divide into 4 equal balls and put one inside each zucchini flower, pinching the tops to make them into little bundles.

Put the flour, cornstarch and a pinch of salt in a bowl, then gradually whisk in enough of the soda club to create a light batter.

Heat the peanut oil in a deep, heavy pot to 350°F, when a cube of day-old bread will brown in 40 seconds. Dip the zucchini flowers into the batter, then deep-fry, in batches if necessary, for about 2 minutes until crisp and golden. Drain well on paper towels and season lightly with salt and pepper before serving.

Serves 4
Preparation time: 15 minutes, plus cooling
Cooking time: 45 minutes

3 skinless boneless chicken thighs
1¾ cups arugula leaves, chopped
1 cup shredded buffalo mozzarella
¼ cup cream cheese
2 tablespoons chopped chives
4 large zucchini flowers
peanut oil, for deep-frying
sea salt and freshly ground black pepper

FOR THE TEMPURA BATTER
¾ cup self-rising flour
1 tablespoon cornstarch
½ to ¾ cup cold soda club

Chicken liver & sweet wine jellied pâté

Chicken liver has a delicate flavor and soft texture that makes a subtle introduction to any meal, and here it is made into a particularly creamy parfait. The contrast with the sweet jello and the slight sharpness of the orange zest set the flavors off perfectly.

Lightly oil a 7- or 8-inch round cake pan and line it with plastic wrap. Melt half the clarified butter in a skillet over medium heat. Add the shallots and fry 3 minutes until just browned, then tip into a blender.

Reheat the skillet, add the remaining clarified butter and the livers and cook 2 minutes on each side until browned on the outside but still just pink in the center. Scrape the livers and butter into the blender containing the shallots.

Return the skillet to the heat and carefully add the brandy. Don't stand too close as it is could catch fire. Deglaze the pan by stirring to remove any caramelized bits stuck to the bottom, then scrape everything into the blender with the other ingredients. Add the cream and season well with salt and pepper. Blitz until gently pureed. With the blender running, gradually add the butter, a piece at a time, until it is all combined. Spoon the mixture into the prepared pan, cover with plastic wrap and chill at least 4 hours in the refrigerator until set. Put the grapes on a baking sheet and freeze at least 2 hours.

Once the parfait is just set, make the jello. Put the gelatin sheets in a bowl of cold water and leave to soak for a few minutes until soft. Put the wine in a pot over low heat to warm through—you don't want it to boil—then remove from the heat and add the orange zest. Slowly and gently whisk in the gelatin sheets one at a time. Transfer to a jug and let cool 5 to 10 minutes. Gently pour the sweet wine jelly on top of the parfait, then cover and return it to the refrigerator at least 2 hours to set.

To serve, gently loosen the plastic wrap around the edges and turn the parfait out onto a cutting board. Cut into cake-style wedges using a knife dipped in boiling water, then serve with fresh bread or toast, and the frozen grapes.

Serves 4 to 6
Preparation time: 30 minutes, plus at least 6 hours chilling, and making the butter
Cooking time: 20 minutes

a little oil, for greasing
3½ tablespoons Clarified Butter (see page 196)
¼ cup thinly sliced shallots
12 ounces chicken livers (about 1½ cups), trimmed
1 tablespoon brandy
1 tablespoon heavy cream
scant 1 cup unsalted butter, softened and cubed
30 green or red seedless grapes, cut into bunches of 5
1½ envelops gelatin
scant ⅔ cup sweet muscat wine
grated zest of 1 orange
sea salt and freshly ground black pepper
fresh bread or toast, to serve

Potted chicken & spiced butter with caramelized shallot jam

The traditional British method called "potting" might sound a bit old-fashioned but don't be fooled—this brings it alive with a contemporary twist of nutmeg and cayenne plus a lovely, sticky-sweet preserve. Not only are potted dishes a useful way to preserve meat, they are ideal if you want an appetizer that you can make ahead of time. I use confit chicken as it is very soft and delicate and works perfectly, set in the spiced butter.

First, make the spiced butter, Melt the butter in a pot over low heat. Remove from the heat and let it settle, then gently pour off the clear butter into a measuring jug, making sure you leave behind the white fats floating on the top or at the bottom. Stir in the nutmeg, cayenne and mace, then set aside.

Put the shredded meat in a bowl, mix in the parsley, and season with salt and pepper to taste. Divide the mixture into four ramekins, filling them just over half full, then slowly pour the spiced butter over the top to cover. Place on a tray and chill about 1 hour in the refrigerator.

To make the shallot jam, heat the oil in a large pot over medium heat, add the shallots and fry 3 to 4 minutes until softened. Add the vinegar, sugar and thyme, and scant ½ cup water, bring to a boil, then turn the heat down to low and simmer about 10 minutes, stirring occasionally, until reduced, thickened and slightly caramelized. Serve the potted chicken with a spoonful of shallot jam and fresh crusty rolls.

Serves 4
Preparation time: 15 minutes, plus 1 hour chilling, and making the confit
Cooking time: 20 minutes

FOR THE SPICED BUTTER
1 cup unsalted butter
½ teaspoon grated nutmeg
a small pinch of cayenne pepper
a small pinch of ground mace

FOR THE CHICKEN
1 confit chicken leg (see page 122), boned and shredded
1 tablespoon chopped parsley leaves
sea salt and freshly ground black pepper
4 homemade or store-bought crusty rolls, toasted, to serve

FOR THE CARAMELIZED SHALLOT JAM
1 tablespoon olive oil
3 cups thinly sliced banana shallots
2 teaspoons red wine vinegar
2 tablespoons dark brown sugar
1 teaspoon chopped thyme leaves

Chicken & shrimp dumplings with soy dipping sauce

I've always been a "grazer" (it stems from tasting lots of dishes while working in the kitchen and generally not having time for proper sit-down meals), so this is just the dish for me—these little dumplings make healthy snack food that's perfect for sharing with friends. If you use a bamboo steamer, you can serve the dumplings right from the steamer.

Mix together the chicken, shrimp, salt and pepper in a bowl. Add all the remaining dumpling filling ingredients, except the wrappers, and mix together. Cover the bowl with plastic wrap and chill 30 minutes in the refrigerator to firm up.

Put a teaspoonful of filling on the first wonton wrapper, bring up the sides and press them around the filling mixture. Tap the dumpling on a flat surface to make the bottom flat, then repeat the process until you have used all the mixture.

Put a large pot of water on to simmer, with a steamer insert on top. Put the dumplings into the steamer and cook 5 to 10 minutes until tender and cooked through.

Meanwhile, mix together all the dipping sauce ingredients in a nonmetallic bowl.

Serve the dumplings right from the steamer, with the dipping sauce served separately.

Serves 4
Preparation time: 20 minutes, plus 30 minutes chilling
Cooking time: 10 minutes

FOR THE CHICKEN & SHRIMP DUMPLINGS
heaped 1 cup ground chicken
9 ounces raw peeled tiger shrimp, finely chopped (about 1½ cups)
1 teaspoon salt
1 teaspoon freshly ground black pepper
¼ cup chopped cilantro leaves
¾ cup water chestnuts, finely chopped
2 tablespoons soy sauce
2 tablespoons finely chopped scallions
1 tablespoon mirin
1 teaspoon sugar
2 teaspoons sesame oil
7 ounces wonton wrappers

FOR THE SOY DIPPING SAUCE
¼ cup light soy sauce
¼ cup Chinese rice vinegar
4 teaspoons toasted sesame oil
2 tablespoons finely chopped cilantro leaves

Chicken meatballs with lime leaf, cardamom & coconut dipping sauce

The influence of Indonesian chicken satay was the starting point for this dish, married with the fact that I enjoy deep-fried meat with a simple sauce. You can also serve the sauce with simple pan-grilled or barbecued chicken.

Heat the oil in a large pot over medium heat. Add the chicken and fry 1 to 2 minutes on each side until browned. Add the broth and bring to a boil, then turn the heat down to low and simmer 2 hours until the meat is falling off the bone. Drain and set aside to dry.

To make the sauce, heat the sesame oil in a pot over medium heat, add the garlic and chilies, then all the spices and cook 2 to 3 minutes, stirring continuously. Stir in the peanuts, then the coconut cream, ginger and sugar, and cook, stirring regularly, for about 15 minutes until thick and well blended. (You can make it ahead of time and store in a screw-top jar in the refrigerator until needed.)

To make the batter, mix together the flour and cornstarch in a bowl, then gradually whisk in the sparkling water until you have a light batter, the consistency of lightly whipped cream. Season with salt and pepper and set aside.

Shred the chicken and mix with the scallions and mustard, season with salt and pepper, and shape into balls about 1½ inches in diameter. Heat the peanut oil in a pot to 350°F, when a cube of bread browns in 50 seconds. One at a time, dip 4 meatballs into the batter and gently lower into the hot oil. Cook about 2 minutes, turning occasionally to cook evenly, then remove from the pot, using a slotted spoon, and drain on paper towels. Keep them warm while you cook the remaining meatballs.

To give the presentation something a little bit special after deep-frying, skewer the meatballs through the center with a bamboo toothpick, keeping the stick exposed on both sides. Put the coconut dipping sauce in a shot glass and sit your skewer on top of the glass.

Serves 4
Preparation time: 30 minutes,
  plus making the broth
Cooking time: 2½ hours

2 tablespoons olive oil
6 skinless chicken thighs
generous 2 cups Chicken Broth
  (see page 197)
2 tablespoons chopped scallions
1 tablespoon Dijon mustard
2 cups peanut oil, for deep-frying
sea salt and freshly ground black pepper

FOR THE COCONUT DIPPING SAUCE
2 tablespoons sesame oil
5 garlic cloves, finely chopped
2 red chilies, seeded and chopped
1 teaspoon finely chopped lemongrass stalk
2 kaffir lime leaves, finely chopped
1 black cardamom pod, crushed to a powder
1 teaspoon ground cumin
2/3 cup unsalted shelled roasted peanuts
1½ cups coconut cream
1 teaspoon peeled and grated ginger root
2 teaspoons sugar

FOR THE BATTER
3/4 cup self-rising flour
1/4 cup cornstarch
2/3 to 3/4 cup cold sparkling water

Chicken, corn & shrimp balls

Chicken, corn and shrimp make a great combination, especially in these crunchy meatballs created by egg-washing and breadcrumbing the meat mixture—add a spicy chili sauce and you have a great dish.

Put the chicken and shrimps into a blender and pulse until minced, then turn into a bowl. Add all the other meatball ingredients and combine together. Cover with plastic wrap and chill 30 minutes in the refrigerator.

Divide and shape the mixture into 8 balls. Whisk together the eggs and milk in a shallow bowl to make an egg wash and put the breadcrumbs in a second bowl. Dip the meatballs in the egg wash, shake off any excess, then roll in the breadcrumbs.

Heat the peanut oil in a deep, heavy pot to 350°F, when a cube of bread browns in 50 seconds. Gently lower the meatballs into the oil, a few at a time, and deep-fry 2 to 3 minutes, turning occasionally so they cook evenly, then remove from the pan, using a slotted spoon, and drain on paper towels. Keep them warm while you cook the remaining meatballs.

Serve the meatballs with sweet chili sauce and a red onion, chive and tomato salad.

Serves 4
Preparation time: 20 minutes, plus 30 minutes chilling
Cooking time: 15 minutes

FOR THE CHICKEN, CORN & SHRIMP MEATBALLS
2 skinless chicken breasts
2 skinless boneless chicken thighs
6 ounces raw peeled tiger shrimps
3/4 cup drained canned corn kernels
4 scallions, finely chopped
2 red chilies
1 lemongrass stalk, finely chopped
1 tablespoon peeled and finely chopped ginger root
2 tablespoons panko breadcrumbs
1 tablespoon chopped cilantro leaves
1 tablespoon chopped chives
1 egg
1 tablespoon olive oil

FOR THE COATING
2 eggs
2 tablespoons milk
1 cup panko breadcrumbs

peanut oil, for deep-frying
1 recipe quantity Sweet Chili Sauce (see page 161), to serve
red onion, chive and tomato salad, to serve

Vietnamese chicken & pomegranate seed wraps with sweet chili sauce

Asian-style finger food makes a sociable and deliciously relaxed way to start any meal. The chicken leg meat gives a great depth of flavor and I like the fact that it remains moist and doesn't dry out when cooking. Crisp bean sprouts, aromatic cilantro and the unusual addition of crunchy pomegranate seeds complete this winning dish.

Heat the oven to 350°F. Heat the oil in a skillet over medium-high heat. Season the chicken with salt and pepper, then add to the pan and fry 1 to 2 minutes on each side until browned. Transfer to a roasting pan and roast 12 minutes until the juices run clear when the thickest part of the chicken is pierced with the tip of a sharp knife. Remove from the oven and let cool slightly, then remove all the meat from the bones, chop finely, then put the meat in a bowl.

Mix together the bean sprouts, chili, cucumber, carrot, scallions and cilantro in another bowl. Hold the pomegranate halves over the bowl and bash the outer skin with a wooden spoon until all the seeds fall into the bowl.

Add the sesame oil and soy sauce, then season with salt and pepper and mix together until combined.

Submerge the rice paper wrappers in warm water and let soak for 1 minute, then lay them out on a board. Take care as they are quite fragile. Put 1 to 2 spoonfuls of the pomegranate mixture and the chicken down the center of a wrapper. Fold the wrapper over the filling, tuck in the ends, then roll the wrapper until it forms a spring roll shape. Continue until you have used all the wrappers and filling mixtures.

Mix together the ingredients for the chili dipping sauce and serve with the wraps. Then just dig in and enjoy your delicious creation.

Serves 4 to 5
Preparation time: 30 minutes
Cooking time: 15 minutes

1 tablespoon olive oil
4 chicken drumsticks
2 cups bean sprouts
1 chili, seeded and cut into thin strips (optional)
½ English cucumber, cut into matchsticks
1 carrot, peeled and sliced into matchsticks
4 scallions, thinly sliced into rings
¼ cup finely chopped cilantro leaves
1 pomegranate, cut in half
1 teaspoon sesame oil
1 teaspoon light soy sauce
8 rice-paper wrappers
sea salt and freshly ground black pepper

FOR THE SWEET CHILI SAUCE
¼ cup light soy sauce
2 teaspoons rice vinegar
1 teaspoon sugar
½ teaspoon peeled and finely grated ginger root
½ teaspoon dried red pepper flakes
1 teaspoon sesame seeds

Chicken in phyllo cones with orange salad

This is an impressive way of presenting a simple salad by filling crisp phyllo pastry cones with chicken meat and serving them with a tangy orange salad. It makes a delightful appetizer or even a summer lunch, or you could make smaller cones and serve as stylish canapés.

Cut a 10-inch circle out of thin card, roll into a cone shape and secure with staples to make a mold. Wrap the mold in aluminum foil, then remove the card and repeat to make 3 more foil cones.

Slice off the top and bottom of the oranges, then peel from top to bottom, using a small, sharp knife, to remove all the skin and the white pith, leaving you with the orange still in shape but without its skin. Holding the orange in one hand, you'll see the lines of the segments. Carefully slice lengthwise on the inside of one of the lines to the center, then the same on the other side of the segment. The segment will just fall out. Repeat this with the whole of both oranges, reserving the juice.

Heat the oven to 350°F. Use 2 sheets of phyllo pastry to wrap a double layer of phyllo around each cone, brushing with melted clarified butter where the sheets overlap. Brush with melted clarified butter and sprinkle with black sesame seeds. Put on a cookie sheet and bake about 4 minutes until golden and cooked. Remove from the oven and let cool before removing the foil cone.

Mix together the chicken, mayonnaise, chives and 1 tablespoon of the reserved orange juice in a bowl, and season to taste with salt and pepper.

Mix together the orange segments and salad greens, season with salt and pepper and drizzle with a little salad dressing. Carefully fill the phyllo cones with the chicken mixture and serve with the orange salad.

Serves 4
Preparation time: 30 minutes, plus making the confit, butter, mayonnaise and dressing
Cooking time: 5 minutes

2 oranges
8 sheets of phyllo pastry dough
2 tablespoons Clarified Butter (see page 196), melted
2 tablespoons black sesame seeds
3 confit chicken legs (see page 122) or poached chicken breasts (see page 23), shredded
3 tablespoons Mayonnaise (see page 202)
2 tablespoons chopped chives
4 cups baby salad greens
a drizzle of Bean House Salad Dressing (see page 203)
sea salt and freshly ground black pepper

Chicken, goat cheese & red onion tarte tatin

Tarte tatin is a classic French recipe for an apple tart cooked upside-down, supposedly invented when a pie was dropped on the floor. This is my modern twist as it is a savory version that combines mellow goat cheese and sweet red onions.

Roll out the dough on a lightly floured surface until it is about 2 inches larger than a 9-inch ovenproof skillet. Cover with a clean, damp cloth and set aside.

Heat the oven to 350°F. Melt the butter in the skillet over low heat, add the thyme, vinegar and sugar, and cook a few minutes until the sugar has dissolved. Add the onions, cut-side down, and cook 3 to 5 minutes until soft. Arrange the chicken in between the onions and cook 8 to 10 minutes until the chicken is cooked through. Sprinkle with the cheese.

Remove the pan from the heat. Carefully lift the phyllo dough and put it over the top of the chicken mixture, tucking in the sides so nothing escapes. Whisk together the egg and milk to make an egg wash and brush over the phyllo dough, then bake 20 minutes until the pastry is golden brown.

Carefully put a plate, slightly larger than the skillet, on top of the pan, then invert the tart onto the plate so the crust is at the bottom. Serve with buttered potatoes and green vegetables.

Serves 4
Preparation time: 15 minutes, plus
  making the pastry dough (optional)
Cooking time: 35 minutes

8 ounces Rough Puff Pastry (see page 208)
  or puff pastry sheets, thawed if frozen
a little flour, for dusting
3 tablespoons unsalted butter
1 tablespoon thyme leaves
2 tablespoons balsamic vinegar
2/3 cup sugar
8 small red onions, cut in half
2 skinless chicken breasts, thinly sliced
1/2 cup crumbled goat cheese
1 egg
1 tablespoon milk
boiled and buttered new potatoes and
  steamed green vegetables, to serve

Chicken Wellington with honey-roasted root vegetables

I couldn't resist trying a chicken version of that classic, beef Wellington, as pastry and meat are just made to go together. It goes with almost any vegetables, but these honey-roasted root vegetables are my first choice. The fillets that are removed are the thin strips underneath the chicken breasts—use them for another dish.

Heat the oven to 375°F. Rinse and drain the spinach, then put it in a pot with just the water clinging to the leaves. Put over medium heat until softened, then drain.

Quarter the pastry, then roll each piece into an 8-inch diameter circle on a lightly floured surface. Beat together the egg and milk to make an egg wash.

Lay 2 slices of pancetta on the counter, put a chicken breast on top, then one-quarter of the spinach and wrap the pancetta tightly around the chicken. Put the wrapped chicken breast on the pastry, brush the edges with egg wash and roll the dough around the chicken, sealing the edges and making sure there are no gaps. Repeat to make the remaining chicken Wellingtons.

Put the chicken Wellingtons on a cookie sheet, brush with the egg wash all over and bake 25 to 30 minutes until cooked through.

Let the Wellingtons rest for 2 minutes, then serve with the roasted vegetables and a little gravy or sauce.

Serves 4
Preparation time: 30 minutes, plus
   making the pastry dough (optional)
Cooking time: 30 minutes

4 cups spinach leaves
7 ounces Rough Puff Pastry (see page 208)
   or puff pastry, thawed if frozen
a little flour, for dusting
1 egg
1 teaspoon milk
8 slices of pancetta
4 skinless chicken breasts, fillets removed
1 recipe quantity Honey-Roasted Root
   Vegetables (see page 216)
1 recipe quantity Traditional Chicken
   Gravy or Red Wine Sauce (see page 198),
   to serve

Chicken, mushroom & red parsley suet pudding

A suet pudding is a hearty English dish, but for my modern version, I am using a lighter chicken filling rather than the traditional steak and kidney. I've given the dough an added boost with a touch of mustard and some Japanese red parsley, or mitsuba, which has a flavor something like celery (and is not actually red.) If you cannot find it, just use flat-leaf parsley instead.

Season the flour with salt and pepper, then coat the chicken in the flour. Melt the butter in a heavy pot over low heat. Add the chicken and fry 2 to 3 minutes on each side until lightly browned. Remove from the pan and set aside.

Heat the oil in the same pan over high heat, add the onion and fry 3 to 4 minutes, then add the garlic and mushrooms and fry 1 minute, stirring. Return the chicken to the pan and add the herbs and broth. Bring to a boil, then reduce the heat to low, cover the pan and simmer 1½ hours until the chicken is tender and the sauce is thick. Let cool.

To make the suet dough, combine all the dry ingredients in a bowl, then gradually add scant ¾ cup water and bring together to a dough. Knead gently on a lightly floured surface 1 minute until smooth.

Bring a pot of water to a boil, with a steamer insert on top, and butter a 6½-inch heatproof round bowl. Roll out the dough on a lightly floured surface into a circle about twice the size of the basin. Cut off a piece to make the lid. Gently fold the larger piece into quarters, then lower it into the basin and open it out so it lines the basin and overhangs the edges. Fill the basin with the chicken and mushrooms. Cut the remaining dough into a circle, dampen the edges and seal to the top of the pudding by pinching the edges together. Trim off any excess. Cover the top with a circle of pleated parchment paper tied with string. Steam 2 hours until cooked through, topping up with boiling water as necessary. Let rest 10 to 15 minutes.

Serve the suet pudding with buttered carrots.

Serves 4
Preparation time: 20 minutes, plus
   30 minutes cooling, and making
   the broth
Cooking time: 3 hours 40 minutes

1 tablespoon all-purpose flour
1¼ pounds skinless boneless chicken
   thighs, cut into small pieces
3½ tablespoons unsalted butter, plus
   extra for greasing
1 tablespoon olive oil
1 large onion, finely chopped
1 large garlic clove, finely chopped
6 ounces crimini mushrooms, cut in half
½ tablespoons chopped thyme leaves
1 bay leaf
scant ⅔ cup Chicken Broth (see page 197)
sea salt and freshly ground black pepper
1 recipe quantity Buttered Carrots
   (see page 216), to serve

FOR THE SUET PASTRY DOUGH
2½ cups self-rising flour, plus extra for
   dusting
1¼ cups chopped suet
2 tablespoons chopped Japanese red
   parsley or flat-leaf parsley
½ teaspoon mustard powder

Spiced pumpkin & chicken pithivier

A pithivier is a round, double-crusted pie usually made with puff pastry dough, marked with a pattern on top and given a high glaze with egg wash. For this version, however, I took an element from the sweet American pumpkin pie and came up with this mildly spicy curried filling.

Melt butter in a large pot over medium heat. Add the onion and curry powder and fry about 3 minutes until the onions are soft but not browned. Add the pumpkin and cook 1 to 2 minutes, stirring.

Toss the chicken in the cornstarch to coat, then add it to the pot along with the corn, and stir until combined. Add the broth and heat to a simmer, stirring occasionally, then add the cream and cook 6 to 8 minutes longer until the sauce thickens and the juices run clear when the thickest part of the chicken is pierced with the tip of a sharp knife. Season with salt and pepper, cover loosely and let cool, then chill 30 minutes in the refrigerator to firm up.

Heat the oven to 400°F and line a baking sheet with parchment paper. Divide the pastry dough in half, then roll out each piece on a lightly floured surface to a circle about 9 inches in diameter and about ⅛-inch thick. Put one piece on the prepared baking sheet and spread the cool filling over the center of the circle, leaving a 1½-inch gap all the way round the edge. Whisk together the egg and milk to make an egg wash, then brush the edges with the egg wash. Carefully lift the other dough circle and place it over the filled base, gently pressing out the air as you press the edges together to seal. Seal securely and make a pattern by gently pressing all the way around the edge with the tines of a fork. Use a sharp knife to score a pattern on the top of the crust from the center to the edges.

Brush the top with egg wash, then bake 10 minutes. Turn the oven down to 300°F and bake 10 to 15 minutes longer until the crust is golden. If you want a high-shine finish and a really golden color, egg wash the pithivier a second time halfway through cooking. Serve warm with a fresh green salad.

Serves 4
Preparation time: 30 minutes, plus
  30 minutes chilling, and making the
  curry paste, broth and dough (optional)
Cooking time: 30 minutes

3½ tablespoons unsalted butter
1 onion, finely chopped
1 tablespoon Curry Paste (see page 204)
10 ounces peeled, seeded and chopped
  pumpkin (about 3 cups)
2 skinless boneless chicken breasts, cut
  into small pieces
1 teaspoon cornstarch
¾ cup drained canned or thawed frozen
  corn kernels
¾ cup Chicken Broth (see page 197)
scant ½ cup heavy cream
1¼ pounds Rough Puff Pastry (see page
  208) or puff pastry dough, thawed if
  frozen
a little flour, for dusting
1 egg
1 teaspoon milk
sea salt and freshly ground black pepper
1 recipe quantity Green Salad (see page
  219), to serve

Stilton, chicken & artichoke lasagne

Eating lasagne reminds me of growing up, as my mom always had it on the menu at our pub and I loved the rich, meaty sauce she made with the creamy béchamel. I usually precook my lasagne sheets but some just need rinsing in boiling water before assembling the lasagne, so check the instructions on the package. I find they sometimes need a bit more liquid in the sauce, in which case, add a little broth or water.

Bring a large pot of lightly salted water to a boil over high heat. Add the lasagne sheets and cook 10 minutes until just tender, then drain and put in a bowl of ice-cold water to stop them cooking any further. Drain well.

Meanwhile, heat the oil and butter in a large pot over high heat. Add the onion and garlic and fry 2 minutes until softened. Add the bacon and Jerusalem artichokes and cook 4 minutes, stirring occasionally, then add the ground chicken and stir together for 6 to 8 minutes, breaking up the chicken, until it is just starting to brown.

Add the tomato puree, tomato paste and thyme, then the red wine sauce and bring to a boil. Turn the heat down to medium and cook about 15 minutes until the sauce thickens slightly. Stir in the parsley and season with salt and pepper to taste, then remove from the heat.

Heat the oven to 350°F and grease an ovenproof lasagne dish. Crumble the Stilton into the béchamel sauce and warm it through to melt slightly.

Cover the bottom of the prepared dish with one-third of the meat sauce, top with a layer of lasagne sheets and cover with another one-third of the meat sauce, another layer of lasagne sheets and the last layer of meat sauce. Pour the béchamel sauce over the top and finish with the shredded cheese.

Bake about 20 minutes until the lasagne is heated through and the cheese has melted and browned slightly on top. Serve with a fresh salad and garlic bread.

Serves 4 to 6
Preparation time: 30 minutes,
  plus making the sauce
Cooking time: 50 minutes

9 ounces lasagne sheets
1 tablespoon olive oil, plus extra for
  greasing
2 tablespoons unsalted butter
1 onion, finely chopped
2 garlic cloves, finely chopped
2 strips smoked bacon, finely chopped
6 ounces Jerusalem artichokes, peeled
  and cut into small cubes
1¼ pounds coarsely ground chicken
1 cup canned tomato puree
2 tablespoons tomato paste
2 tablespoons chopped thyme leaves
1¼ cups Red Wine Sauce (see page 198)
1 tablespoon chopped parsley leaves
½ crumbled Stilton cheese
generous 1¼ cups Béchamel Sauce (see
  page 199)
⅓ cup shredded cheddar cheese
sea salt and freshly ground black pepper
1 recipe quantity Green Salad (see page
  219), to serve
garlic bread, to serve

Asian chicken & mushroom ballotines

Probably the best known of all the chicken flavor combinations, this simple dish really lets the ingredients shine. A boned chicken thigh is stuffed ith forcemeat , then formed into a sausage shape and poached. I have given the dish a distinctly creamy flavor and combined that with earthy wild mushrooms and a touch of Asia with the spiced rice.

To make the stuffing, put the chicken pieces in a blender and blend until smooth. Gradually pour in the cream while pulsing the blender. Transfer the mixture to a bowl, season with salt and pepper, then cover and chill in the refrigerator.

Heat the butter in a skillet and fry the mushrooms 5 minutes until soft. Stir in the curry paste and let cool.

Combine the mushroom and chicken mixtures. Spoon into a disposable pastry bag and chill 30 minutes in the refrigerator to firm up. Pipe the chilled mousse into each boned chicken leg, making sure it fills each one, then pull the skin over the ends to make a sausage shape.

Lay a double layer of plastic wrap on the counter and lay 5 slices of pancetta vertically next to each other (so there are no gaps) across the center, then place the chicken ballotine across the top. Fold the pancetta around the chicken until it is completely enclosed, and tuck in the ends. Roll the plastic wrap around the chicken, pushing out any air as you do so, and tie each end securely in a knot. Repeat with the remaining ballotines.

Bring a large pot of water to a boil over high heat, then turn the heat down to a simmer. Add the ballotines and poach 30 minutes until cooked through. Remove with a slotted spoon and place in a large bowl of cold water 2 to 3 minutes until cool enough to handle.

Heat the oil in a large skillet over medium heat. Remove the ballotines from the water and take off the plastic wrap. Add the ballotines to the pan and fry 2 to 3 minutes, turning occasionally, until browned all over. Slice the ballotines, put on a bed of spiced rice and lentils and scatter with crisp fried shallots before serving.

Serves 4
Preparation time: 45 minutes, plus 30 minutes chilling, and making the curry paste
Cooking time: 40 minutes

7 ounces chicken leg or thigh meat, cut into pieces

scant 1 cup heavy cream

2 tablespoons unsalted butter

3½ ounces wild mushrooms, such as girolles, porcini or morels, sliced

2 tablespoons Curry Paste (see page 204)

4 chicken thighs, skin on, tunnel boned (see page 21)

20 thin slices of pancetta

2 tablespoons olive oil

sea salt and freshly ground black pepper

1 recipe quantity Spiced Rice & Lentils (see page 210), to serve

1 recipe quantity Crisp Fried Shallots (see page 205), to serve

Medallions of chicken, peas & fava beans in tarragon cream

One of the first dishes I ever cooked was chicken breast with a cream and tarragon sauce. The flavors of tarragon, cream and chicken are just perfect together, especially when combined with the contrasting crunch of fresh peas and fava beans to make a delicious dinner. By cutting the chicken into medallions, it makes the recipe very quick while the chicken still remains tender. Fava beans are available from Indian and Middle Eastern stores.

Heat 1 teaspoon of the oil and the butter in a skillet over medium-high heat. Add the onion and garlic and fry 1 to 2 minutes until softened. Add the broth and cream and simmer 5 minutes until the liquid has reduced by half. Add the peas, beans and tarragon, and stir well, then remove from the heat.

Meanwhile, put the rice in a pot and add enough water to come about ¾ inch above the rice. Bring to a boil over high heat and cook about 5 minutes until almost all the water has evaporated. Turn the heat down as low as it will go, cover with a lid and let the rice steam gently about 5 minutes until it is tender but not soft, and is still holding its shape. Remove the pan from the heat. Keep the pan covered so the rice stays warm and set aside until needed.

Heat the remaining oil in a large skillet. Season the chicken with salt and pepper, then add to the pan and fry 2 to 3 minutes on each side until golden and cooked through. Remove the chicken from the pan and set aside.

Add the sauce to the chicken skillet and cook over high heat for about 5 minutes until the sauce just starts to thicken slightly.

Stir the chives into the rice and season with salt and pepper to taste. Serve the chicken on top of the rice with the sauce spooned over the top.

Serves 4
Preparation time: 15 minutes, plus making the broth
Cooking time: 25 minutes

1 tablespoon olive oil
1 teaspoon unsalted butter
1 red onion, finely chopped
1 garlic clove, chopped
¾ cup Chicken or Vegetable Broth (see page 197)
¾ cup heavy cream
⅔ cup shelled or frozen peas, thawed if frozen
¾ cup shelled fava beans
2 tablespoons chopped tarragon leaves
1⅔ cups basmati rice, rinsed
4 skinless chicken breasts, cut across into medallions
2 tablespoons chopped chives
sea salt and freshly ground black pepper

Smoked chicken & wild garlic risotto

Once you master the basics of risotto, the options are endless. You can also make the base ahead of time, then finish it off just before serving—perfect when you are in a rush. If you can't find wild garlic, or it's out of season (spring to early summer), just use baby leaf spinach. And do have a go at smoking the chicken yourself (see page 144).

Heat the oil and butter in a large skillet over medium heat. Add the onion and garlic and fry 5 minutes, stirring occasionally, until softened. Stir in the rice to coat it in the onion mixture. Pour in the wine and stir until it is absorbed by the rice.

Add a small ladleful of the hot broth and stir until the broth is absorbed by the rice before adding the next ladleful. Keep stirring the rice to prevent it sticking and to make sure it cooks evenly. Continue adding the broth until you have used half of it; this should take about 10 minutes. This is the risotto base and it can be left at this stage, if more convenient, and the dish finished later. If you want to do this, transfer the rice to a container with a lid and let cool completely. When cool, cover and chill up to 2 days.

To finish the risotto, reheat the reserved broth, if necessary. Return the rice to the large skillet over a medium-low heat. Continue to add the broth a ladleful at a time as before, stirring continuously, until the broth is absorbed and the rice is tender but still retains some bite; this will take about 10 minutes. Make sure the rice is piping hot, if reheating it.

Add the chicken, cream, Parmesan, lemon juice, wild garlic and chives. Season with salt and pepper to taste and stir until well combined and heated through. Serve the risotto sprinkled with extra Parmesan.

Serves 4
Preparation time: 20 minutes,
 plus making the broth
Cooking time: 35 minutes

FOR THE RISOTTO BASE
1 tablespoon olive oil
$1/3$ cup unsalted butter
1 large onion, finely chopped
2 garlic cloves, finely chopped
$1^1/3$ cups risotto rice, such as arborio
scant 1 cup dry white wine
$3^1/4$ cups hot Vegetable Broth
 (see page 197)

FOR THE WILD GARLIC BUTTER
4 wild garlic leaves, finely chopped
2 wild garlic bulbs, finely chopped
1 cup unsalted butter

FOR THE SMOKED CHICKEN RISOTTO
4 smoked chicken breasts (see page 144),
 skin-on, or roasted chicken breasts (see
 page 23), skinned, boned and shredded
scant $1/2$ cup heavy cream
2 cups shredded parmesan cheese, plus
 extra for serving
juice of $1/2$ lemon
1 large handful of wild garlic leaves or
 baby spinach leaves, roughly chopped
1 tablespoon chopped chives
sea salt and freshly ground black pepper

Malaysian chicken rendang

This dish is bursting with the traditional Thai flavors of chili, fresh ginger, lemongrass and coconut milk. In my new version, you make a paste from the flavoring ingredients, then cook the meat slowly to intensify the flavors.

Heat the oven to 315°F. Put all the curry paste ingredients in a blender, season with salt and pepper and blitz together to a paste.

Heat the oil in a stovetop and ovenproof dish over medium heat, add the chicken and fry a few minutes until lightly browned. Add the spice paste, bring to a boil, then cover with a lid, transfer to the oven and bake 1½ hours until cooked through and completely tender.

Scatter with the cilantro and serve with boiled rice.

Serves 4
Preparation time: 15 minutes
Cooking time: 1½ hours

1 tablespoon olive oil
4 chicken thighs, skin on
4 chicken drumsticks, skin on
2 tablespoons chopped cilantro leaves
sea salt and freshly ground black pepper
boiled rice, to serve

FOR THE CURRY PASTE
1½ onions, quartered
1 tablespoon ground coriander
2 lemongrass stalks, finely chopped
4 red chilies, seeded and chopped
1 tablespoon ground cumin
1 tablespoon dark brown sugar
2 tablespoons peeled and grated ginger
  root
3 garlic cloves
1¾ cups coconut milk
1 teaspoon Thai fish sauce
1 star anise, ground to a fine powder

Chicken rogan josh with fenugreek potatoes

Homemade curry is rather special but can take a bit of time, so I've used a curry paste that you can keep in the refrigerator to make things a bit easier when you want a quick meal. Rogan josh has a lovely rich tomato sauce with loads of flavor.

Heat 1 tablespoon of the oil and the butter in a large, heavy pot over high heat. Add the chicken and fry 3 minutes on each side until sealed. Remove from the pan and set aside until needed.

Heat the remaining oil in the same pan over low heat. Add the onions and garlic and fry 8 minutes until softened and just starting to color. Add the cardamom pods, cinnamon stick and curry paste, and stir well, then stir in the tomatoes, tomato paste, sugar and broth. Turn the heat up to high and bring to a boil, then turn the heat down to low, cover with a lid and simmer 1 to 1½ hours until the chicken is tender and almost falling apart.

When the chicken is almost ready, heat the oil and butter for the potatoes in a skillet over medium-high heat. Add the potatoes, sprinkle with the fenugreek seeds and stir together for a few minutes until hot.

Sprinkle the curry with the cilantro and serve with the fenugreek potatoes and an onion and mint salad.

Serves 4
Preparation time: 20 minutes, plus making the curry paste and broth
Cooking time: 1¾ hours

3 tablespoons olive oil
1 tablespoon unsalted butter
8 skinless boneless chicken thighs
2 onions, thinly sliced
2 garlic cloves, finely chopped
2 black cardamom pods
1 cinnamon stick
¼ cup Curry Paste (see page 204)
1½ cups canned crushed tomatoes
⅓ cup tomato paste
1 teaspoon dark brown sugar
1¾ cups Chicken Broth (see page 197)
1 to 2 tablespoons cilantro leaves
sliced onion and mint salad, to serve

FOR THE FENUGREEK POTATOES
1 tablespoon olive oil
1 tablespoon unsalted butter
7 ounces cooked new potatoes
2 teaspoons ground fenugreek seeds

Persian chicken

Persian cooking is about zingy flavors, often combining sweet and savory in the traditional Middle Eastern style, with lots of citrus tang. You'll find sumac with the spices in major supermarkets or in ethnic stores—it adds to the citrus notes in this dish.

Heat the oven to 315°F and have ready a large ovenproof dish. Put the saffron strands in a small bowl, pour over 2 tablespoons hot water and let stand.

Heat 1 tablespoon of the clarified butter in a large skillet over medium-high heat. Add the chicken in two batches and fry each batch for 10 minutes until all sides are caramelized and nicely colored. Remove the chicken from the pan and set aside.

Heat the remaining clarified butter and fry the cardamom pods, cinnamon, cloves and bay leaves for 1 minute until fragrant. Add the onions, season with salt and pepper and cook over low heat for 5 to 10 minutes, stirring occasionally, until they start to caramelize.

Stir in the rice, dates, raisins, almonds and pistachios and ensure they are all mixed together thoroughly. Stir in 2¾ cups water, the orange, lemon and lime zest, and the sumac, and bring to a simmer.

Tip the rice mixture into the casserole dish, drizzle the saffron water over it and bury the chicken thighs in the rice. Cover with aluminum foil and bake 20 to 25 minutes until the water has evaporated, the rice is tender and the chicken juices run clear when the thickest part of the chicken is pierced with the tip of a sharp knife. Sprinkle with the cilantro and serve.

Serves 4
Preparation time: 15 minutes,
  plus making the butter
Cooking time: 50 minutes

a good pinch of saffron strands
¼ cup Clarified Butter (see page 196)
12 boneless chicken thighs, skin on
12 cardamom pods, crushed
2 large cinnamon sticks
4 cloves
2 dried bay leaves
2 onions, thinly sliced
1¾ cups basmati rice, rinsed
10 dates, pitted and sliced
2 tablespoons raisins
2 tablespoons toasted slivered almonds
2 tablespoons shelled pistachios
2 strips of orange zest
2 strips of lemon zest
2 strips of lime zest
2 tablespoons sumac
2 tablespoons cilantro leaves
sea salt and freshly ground black pepper

Chicken bourguignon

A take on comfort food at its best, this classic dish is cooked slowly so the meat is bathed in a rich sauce flavored with smoked bacon and mushrooms. Serve it with plenty of creamy mashed potatoes, and you can't beat it.

Heat the oven to 350°F. Heat 2 tablespoons oil in a large skillet. Add the chicken, in batches if necessary, and fry about 6 minutes until sealed on all sides, then transfer to an ovenproof dish, keeping the skillet to one side.

Put the red wine, sugar and star anise in a pot over high heat, bring to a boil, then boil about 5 minutes until reduced by half.

Put the skillet back on the heat, add the celery, onion, garlic, leek and thyme, and fry 2 to 3 minutes until softened and lightly browned, then add to the casserole dish with the meat.

Pour the reduced wine into the skillet and add the broth. Bring to a boil and deglaze the pan by stirring to remove any caramelized bits stuck to the bottom. Pour into the casserole dish, cover with a lid and transfer to the oven for 1½ hours until the meat is just falling apart.

While the chicken is cooking, bring a large pot of water to a boil over high heat, add the pearl onions and boil 5 minutes until softened, then remove from the water with a slotted spoon, plunge into ice-cold water, then drain and set aside. Return the water to a boil, add the carrots and boil 2 minutes, then remove from the pan, plunge into the ice-cold water, drain and add to the onions. Heat a skillet and fry the bacon until crisp, then chop it and add it to the onions. Stir the mushrooms into the pan and fry 5 minutes until softened, then add to the onions.

When the chicken is cooked, stir in the onion mixture and the parsley, then bake 10 minutes longer. Serve with creamy mashed potatoes.

Serves 4
Preparation time: 1 hour, plus making the broth
Cooking time: 2 hours

2 tablespoons olive oil
12 skinless boneless chicken thighs, cut in half
1 bottle of dry red wine
1 tablespoon dark brown sugar
1 star anise
1 celery stalk, finely chopped
1 onion, finely chopped
2 garlic cloves, finely chopped
1 leek, trimmed and thinly sliced
1 thyme sprig
generous 2 cups Chicken Broth (see page 197)
16 pearl onions or shallots
2 carrots, peeled and chopped
1 teaspoon olive oil
2 strips smoked bacon
4 ounces crimini mushrooms, quartered
1 tablespoon chopped parsley leaves
1 recipe quantity Creamy Mashed Potatoes (see page 212), to serve

Spinach-rolled chicken with onion puree & charred leeks

Rinse and drain the spinach, then put it in a pot with just the water clinging to the leaves. Put over medium heat until softened, then drain.

Put 1 chicken breast in between 2 sheets of parchment paper and gently beat to flatten. Lay a double layer of plastic wrap on the counter, put the flat chicken breast on top, season with salt and pepper and top with some spinach. Roll the chicken to encase the filling, then roll the plastic wrap around the whole thing, pushing out any air, and tie each end securely in a knot. Wrap in the same way with aluminum foil. Repeat with the remaining chicken.

Bring a pot of water to a boil over high heat, then turn the heat down to low, add the chicken and simmer 30 minutes until the juices run clear when the thickest part of the chicken is pierced with the tip of a sharp knife.

At the same time, to make the onion puree, heat the butter in a large pot over medium heat, add the onions and fry about 20 minutes until softened and golden. Season with salt and pepper. Put into a blender and blitz to a puree, adding a little boiling water if the puree is too thick.

Meanwhile, bring a pot of water to a boil over high heat, add the baby leeks and cook 1 minute. Drain and put in a bowl of ice-cold water for 5 minutes, then drain and pat dry.

Put the leeks in a bowl and drizzle with 1 tablespoon of the oil. Heat a ridged grill pan over high heat, add the leeks and cook until they have charred black markings.

Remove the cooked chicken from the water and let rest for 2 minutes before unwrappping. Heat the remaining oil in a skillet, add the chicken and fry on all sides until golden. Slice the chicken into medallions and put on top of the warm onion puree along with the charred leeks. Serve with potato croquettes and wilted greens.

Serves 4
Preparation time: 40 minutes
Cooking time: 40 minutes

4 cups spinach leaves
4 skinless chicken breasts
3½ tablespoons unsalted butter
10 ounces onions or shallots, thinly sliced (about 2⅔ cups)
12 baby leeks, trimmed, or 4 leeks, trimmed and quartered
2 tablespoons olive oil
sea salt and freshly ground black pepper
1 recipe quantity Potato Croquettes (see page 214), to serve
1 recipe quantity Wilted Greens (see page 217), to serve

Chicken in lovage butter en papillote

Cooking en papillote—or in a bundle—is a fantastic way of preparing chicken. It steams all the ingredients together and keeps the chicken lovely and moist, then once the vegetables are cooked, they reduce down and make a juicy broth. Serve these on a plate or boards, still in the paper, so your guests can open their bundle themselves and get the first whiff of the fresh vegetables and herbs with the golden chicken.

Heat the oven to 350°F. Put the potatoes in a pot of water, cover and bring to a boil over high heat. Turn the heat down to medium and cook 10 minutes until tender, then drain and set aside.

Season the chicken with salt and pepper. Heat 1 tablespoon of the oil in a skillet over medium heat, add the chicken and fry a few minutes until just colored on all sides, then remove from the heat.

Mix together the butter, lovage, tarragon and garlic.

Put 4 large sheets of parchment paper on the counter. Divide the samphire, peas, zucchini and tomatoes among the papers, then top each pile with a tablespoon of the herb butter. Put a chicken breast on the vegetables and a teaspoon of butter on top. Season with a little salt and pepper. Bring the edges of the parchment paper up over the ingredients of the first bundle and fold and scrunch the edges together to seal. Repeat to form 3 more bundles and put them in a roasting pan.

Bake the bundles 15 to 20 minutes, then carefully open one to check that the juices run clear when the thickest part of the chicken is pierced with the tip of a sharp knife.

Meanwhile, heat the remaining oil in a skillet over high heat. Add the chorizo and fry a few minutes until browned, then add the potatoes and stir until heated through. Serve the chicken still in the paper so your guests can open their own bundle, along with the potatoes and chorizo.

Serves 4
Preparation time: 20 minutes
Cooking time: 30 minutes

20 baby new potatoes
4 chicken statler breasts or breasts, skin on
3 tablespoons olive oil
generous ½ cup salted butter, softened
3 tablespoons chopped lovage or watercress
1 teaspoon chopped tarragon leaves
2 garlic cloves, crushed
4 ounces salicornia (*pousse pierre*) or tenderstem broccoli
heaped ⅓ cup shelled peas
2 zucchini, roughly chopped
2 large vine tomatoes, chopped, including seeds
½ cup chorizo, thinly sliced
sea salt and freshly ground black pepper

Chicken with fig & goat cheese wrapped in prosciutto

This is such a simple recipe but so effective and delicious that it can take center stage at your next dinner party for friends. The stuffing and the prosciutto wrapping both help to keep the meat beautifully moist as well as imparting plenty of flavor.

Heat the oven to 400°F. Make a horizontal slit down each chicken breast, making sure you don't cut right through. Open up the chicken breasts as flat as possible and place each one on 2 slices of prosciutto.

Mix together the figs and goat cheese, then put one-quarter of the mixture on each chicken breast and season with salt and pepper. Fold the chicken over the filling, then wrap the prosciutto around the outside and secure with toothpicks, if necessary.

Heat the oil in a skillet, add the chicken breasts and cook 2 minutes on each side until browned, then transfer to a roasting pan and roast 15 minutes until the juices run clear when the thickest part of the chicken is pierced with the tip of a sharp knife.

Serve hot with a fresh salad and buttered new potatoes.

Serves 4
Preparation time: 15 minutes
Cooking time: 20 minutes

4 skinless chicken breasts
8 slices prosciutto
8 fresh figs, sliced
½ cup crumbled soft goat cheese
1 tablespoon olive oil
sea salt and freshly ground black pepper
1 recipe quantity Green Salad (see page 219) or a mixed leaf salad, to serve
boiled and buttered new potatoes, to serve

Asian-style chicken Kiev

I'm sure everyone at some point has eaten a chicken Kiev, a classic combination of chicken rolled or stuffed with garlic butter and herbs, then breaded and fried, or baked in the oven. There is dispute as to whether it was created in Russia, in Paris, or actually in Kiev, the capital of the Ukraine, but it certainly gained popularity in the 1970s and became a classic recipe for restaurants and one of the original British supermarket ready-meals. But giving it an Asian twist changes the style and brings it right up to date, lifting the rather predictable flavors to give a fantastic, pungent and spicy chicken dish.

Beat the softened butter in a mixing bowl for 30 seconds. Mix in the lime zest and juice, the mint, cilantro, garlic and ginger, and season with salt and pepper. Mix thoroughly, then cover and chill about 1 hour in the refrigerator, if you can, for the flavors to develop. Remove from the refrigerator to soften just before you are ready to use it.

Using a small, very sharp knife, make a slit in the flesh of each breast fillet from top to bottom, creating a pocket at a slight angle. Spoon the butter mixture into a pastry bag with a large plain tip and pipe into the pocket.

Put the cornstarch in a shallow bowl and season with salt and pepper. Tip the beaten eggs into another shallow bowl, and the breadcrumbs into a third. Toss the stuffed chicken breasts first in the flour to coat, shaking off any excess, then slide them one at a time into the egg, and turn until covered. Finally, dip each one into the breadcrumbs, again shaking off any excess. Lay the breasts, slit sides down, on a plate, cover and chill at least 30 minutes in the refrigerator to help firm the crumb coating.

When ready to cook, heat the oven to 375°F. Heat the oil in an ovenproof skillet over medium heat until you can feel a good heat rising. Add the chicken breasts and fry 1 to 2 minutes on each side until lightly golden. Transfer the pan to the oven and cook 12 to 14 minutes until golden brown and the juices run clear when the thickest part of the chicken is pierced with the tip of a sharp knife. Spoon any butter from the roasting pan over them, and serve hot with roast potatoes and green beans.

Serves 4
Preparation time: 25 minutes,
  plus 1½ hours chilling
Cooking time: 16 minutes

¾ cup unsalted butter, softened
grated zest and juice of 1 lime
leaves from 6 mint sprigs, roughly
  chopped
2 handfuls of cilantro leaves and stalks
3 large garlic cloves, finely chopped
2½-inch piece of ginger root, peeled
  and finely chopped
4 skinless chicken breasts
1 cup cornstarch
2 large eggs, beaten
1 cup panko breadcrumbs
3 tablespoons sunflower oil
sea salt and freshly ground black pepper
1 recipe quantity Roast Potatoes
  (see page 212), to serve
steamed green beans, to serve

Grilled chicken tikka on lemongrass sticks

Chicken tikka is one of our most popular dishes and when you use lemongrass as the kebab skewers, you get another layer of flavor coming into the mix. If you don't have any, though, you can simply use ordinary metal or soaked wooden skewers.

Mix together all the marinade ingredients in a nonmetallic baking tray. Thread the chicken onto the lemongrass stalks and put in the tray, turning to coat the meat. Cover with plastic wrap and let marinate in the refrigerator 2 hours.

Meanwhile, mix the onion, Belgian endive leaves and tomatoes in a bowl. Whisk together the lemon juice and oil, then drizzle it over the salad, cover with plastic wrap and chill in the refrigerator until ready to serve.

Heat the barbecue or a large ridged grill pan and cook the chicken for about 10 minutes, turning frequently, until the juices run clear when the thickest part of the chicken is pierced with the tip of a sharp knife.

Serve the chicken with the onion and tomato salsa and some nan bread.

Serves 4
Preparation time: 20 minutes,
  plus 2 hours marinating
Cooking time: 10 minutes

2¼ pounds skinless boneless chicken
  thighs, cut into cubes
8 lemongrass stalks
1 red onion, thinly sliced
4 Belgian endive heads, separated into
  leaves
4 large vine tomatoes, quartered
juice of ½ lemon
1 tablespoon olive oil
nan bread, to serve

FOR THE MARINADE
½ cup plain yogurt
1 teaspoon peeled and grated ginger root
2 garlic cloves, grated
1 teaspoon mild Madras curry powder
1 teaspoon garam masala
1 teaspoon lemon juice
1 tablespoon tomato paste
2 teaspoons sugar
½ teaspoon chili powder

Golden chicken & mint mojito

A mojito is a classic cocktail—fresh mint from the garden with sharp lime and white rum sweetened with sugar syrup. The combination was too perfect not to use for a recipe since it brings all those elements to lift the chicken, so here is my mojito chicken, using golden rum instead of white for a simple but effective twist. I love this dish cooked on the barbecue for that smoked, charred flavor or, if you are in the kitchen, use a ridged grill pan for a similar effect.

Score the chicken breasts a couple of times across the top and bottom to allow the marinade to penetrate. Put the rum, lime zest and juice, mint, ginger, cilantro and sugar into a small blender or mortar and pestle, and crush to a paste. Rub the marinade into the chicken, put in a nonmetallic bowl, cover and let marinate in the refrigerator at least 2 hours or overnight if possible.

If you are using a barbecue, wait for the charcoal to go white with no naked flames, then cook the chicken breasts for 2 to 3 minutes on each side, then keep turning them and brushing with marinade 5 to 10 minutes longer until the juices from the chicken run clear when the thickest part of the chicken is pierced with the tip of a sharp knife. Baste with plenty of marinade while they are cooking so they don't dry out.

If you are in the kitchen, heat the oven to 400°F. Heat a ridged grill pan over high heat until very hot, then add the chicken breasts and seal for 2 minutes on each side until you have charred stripes on the meat. Transfer to the oven and cook 5 minutes until cooked through and tender. Slice the chicken, scatter with mint leaves and lime wedges, and serve with a fresh, crisp salad and new potatoes.

Serves 4
Preparation time: 10 minutes,
  plus overnight marinating
Cooking time: 20 minutes

4 skinless chicken breasts
1/3 cup golden rum
grated zest and juice of 2 limes
leaves from 12 large mint sprigs, plus
  extra to serve
1/2-inch piece ginger root, peeled and
  chopped
12 large cilantro sprigs, including stalks
2 tablespoons dark brown sugar
2 limes, cut into wedges
1 recipe quantity Green Salad
  (see page 219), to serve
boiled new potatoes, to serve

Barbecued garlic & thyme spring chicken with celery root, beet & sunflower seed coleslaw

If you are feeling very confident with a knife, you can cut the celery root and beet into very fine matchsticks. And don't be put off by the idea of spatchcocking the squab chickens—it is really very simple and makes for a dramatic presentation.

Beat together the butter, garlic and thyme until well blended. Rub into the squab chickens, pushing some under the skin of the breast if you can, to help keep the meat moist while it is cooking. Heat the barbecue or oven to maximum.

To make the coleslaw, put the celery root and beets in a bowl and stir in the lemon juice. Add the mayonnaise, crème fraîche, mustards and parsley, and mix well. Add the toasted sunflower seeds and season with salt and pepper to taste. Cover and put in the refrigerator until needed.

Cook the squab chickens over maximum heat on the barbecue 1 to 2 minutes on each side, then transfer to a higher shelf and cook with the lid closed for about 5 to 10 minutes more until the juices run clear when the thickest part of the chicken is pierced with the tip of a sharp knife. Alternatively, cook in the oven for 4 minutes, then turn the oven temperature down to 375°F and cook 10 minutes longer. Let rest for a couple of minutes in a warm place, then serve hot with the coleslaw.

Serves 4
Preparation time: 30 minutes, plus making the mayonnaise
Cooking time: 15 minutes

¼ cup unsalted butter
2 garlic cloves, finely chopped
leaves from 2 thyme sprigs, chopped
4 squab chickens, spatchcocked (see page 20)
½ celery root, peeled and grated
2 beets, peeled and grated
2 teaspoons freshly squeezed lemon juice
¼ cup Mayonnaise (see page 202)
2 tablespoons crème fraîche or sour cream
2 tablespoons Dijon mustard
2 teaspoons wholegrain mustard
2 teaspoons chopped parsley leaves
2 tablespoons sunflower seeds, lightly toasted
sea salt and freshly ground black pepper

Maple & mustard-glazed squab chickens with scallion & lemon couscous

The great thing about squab chickens is that you can cook them on the bone so they stay lovely and moist and, of course, they are perfect for one person. This maple and mustard glaze makes the squab chickens sweet and sticky, counterbalanced by the citrus couscous.

Heat the oven to 350°F. Mix together the maple syrup, mustard, soy sauce and orange juice. Peel 4 garlic cloves and put a garlic clove and a thyme sprig inside each of the squab chickens, then tie the legs together and put them in a roasting pan. Pour the maple syrup mixture over them and stir in the remaining garlic. Roast 20 to 25 minutes, basting occasionally with the syrup, until the squab chickens are cooked through and the juices run clear when a knife is inserted into the thigh.

Meanwhile, bring the broth to a boil in a pot over high heat. Put the couscous in a bowl and pour the broth over it, stirring continuously. Cover with plastic wrap and let stand 15 to 20 minutes until the couscous is tender and has absorbed most of the liquid. Drain off any excess liquid. Stir in the scallions, chives and lemon zest and juice, and season with salt and pepper to taste.

Let the squab chickens rest 3 to 4 minutes, then serve on a bed of lemon couscous.

Serves 4
Preparation time: 15 minutes,
  and making the broth
Cooking time: 25 minutes

⅔ cup maple syrup
¼ cup wholegrain mustard
2 tablespoons light soy sauce
2 tablespoons freshly squeezed
  orange juice
12 unpeeled garlic cloves, flattened
  with a knife
4 thyme sprigs
4 squab chickens
1 cup Chicken Broth (see page 197)
1⅓ cups couscous
6 scallions, thinly sliced
2 tablespoons chopped chives
grated zest and juice of 1 lemon
sea salt and freshly ground black pepper

basic recipes

Clarified butter or ghee

Melt the butter in a small pot over low heat. Alternatively, put it in a clear microwave-safe bowl and melt in the microwave.

Remove from the heat and let settle, then gently pour off the clear butter into a cup, making sure you leave behind the white fats floating on the top or at the bottom.

Store in an airtight container up to a week in the refrigerator.

Makes 1 cup
Preparation time: 2 minutes, plus settling
Cooking time: 2 minutes

1 cup unsalted butter

Herb oil

Bring a pot of water to a boil over high heat and have a bowl of ice-cold water ready. Add the herbs and spinach to the boiling water and blanch for 1 minute, then lift out with a fine-mesh strainer and put into the ice-cold water to stop them cooking any further.

Lift the herbs and spinach out of the ice-cold water and gently shake off any excess, then transfer to a small blender. Add the oil and blitz to a puree, then season with salt and pepper to taste. Pour in an airtight container and leave to infuse in the refrigerator overnight.

Secure a double thickness of cheesecloth over the top of a measuring cup. Pour the oil into the cup through the cheesecloth, then leave it to one side to strain for a few hours, without disturbing it. Discard the solids and pour the clear oil into an airtight container.

Store in an airtight container up to a week in the refrigerator.

Makes about 1 cup
Preparation time: 15 minutes, plus 3 hours straining and overnight infusing
Cooking time: 1 minute

1 teaspoon chopped basil leaves
1 teaspoon chopped chives
2 teaspoons chopped flat-leaf parsley leaves
1 1/2 cups spinach leaves
1 1/4 cups olive oil
sea salt and freshly ground black pepper

Chicken broth

Heat the oven to 400°F. Put the carcasses in a roasting pan and roast 1 hour until browned.

Transfer to a large pot and add all the remaining ingredients and 3 quarts cold water. Bring to a boil over high heat, then turn the heat down as low as possible and simmer gently 1 to 2 hours, skimming occasionally to remove any scum floating to the top.

Remove from the heat, cover and let cool a couple of hours. Strain into a clean pan, discarding the bones and vegetables. Bring to a boil, then boil until reduced to about 4 cups broth.

Store in an airtight container up to 4 days in the refrigerator or freeze in conveniently sized containers.

Makes about 4 cups
Preparation time: 10 minutes, plus 2 hours cooling
Cooking time: 3½ hours

5 pounds chicken carcasses
2 unpeeled onions, quartered
4 carrots, broken in half
1 garlic bulb, cut in half horizontally
2 leeks, trimmed and cut in half
2 celery stalks
2 thyme sprigs
2 small bunches of flat-leaf parsley
2 bay leaves
12 black peppercorns
6 vine tomatoes
2 star anise

Vegetable broth

Put all the ingredients in a large pot over high heat and add 8 cups cold water. Bring to a boil, then turn the heat down to low and simmer 30 minutes.

Let cool, then pour the contents of the pot into a plastic container, cover and store in the refrigerator overnight.

Strain the broth and discard any solids. Store in an airtight container up to a week in the refrigerator or freeze in conveniently sized containers.

Makes about 8 cups
Preparation time: 10 minutes, plus overnight chilling
Cooking time: 40 minutes

3 onions, quartered
4 carrots, chopped
2 leeks, trimmed and chopped
2 celery stalks, chopped
1 garlic bulb, cut in half horizontally
12 black peppercorns
2 star anise
2 tarragon sprigs
2 thyme sprigs
2 parsley sprigs
1 rosemary sprig
1 sage sprig
1 lovage sprig (optional)
2¾ ounces dried wild mushrooms
scant 1 cup white wine

Red wine sauce

Heat the oil in a large pot over medium heat. Add the vegetables and thyme and fry 4 to 5 minutes.

Add the wine and port and deglaze the pan by stirring to remove any caramelized bits stuck to the bottom. Bring to a boil, then simmer to reduce the liquid by half.

Add the broth, red currant jelly and star anise, return to a boil, then simmer about 30 to 40 minutes until the liquid is reduced by about half.

Strain the liquid through a fine mesh strainer, then season with salt and pepper to taste. If you want the sauce to be thicker, put the strained liquid back on the heat, bring to a boil and boil to reduce further until it reaches the thickness you want.

Store in an airtight container up to 4 days in the refrigerator or freeze 1 month in conveniently sized containers.

Makes about 3 cups
Preparation time: 20 minutes, plus making the broth
Cooking time: 1 hour

2 tablespoons olive oil
1 celery stick, chopped
1 leek, trimmed and thinly sliced
1 carrot, peeled and chopped
1 onion, finely chopped
2 thyme sprigs
1½ cups dry red wine
½ cup port
6 cups Chicken Broth (see page 197)
½ cup red currant jelly
1 star anise
sea salt and freshly ground black pepper

Traditional chicken gravy

After you have roasted the chicken, remove it from the roasting pan, cover and leave it in a warm place while you make the gravy.

Put the roasting pan over medium-high heat and bring the juices to a boil. Whisk in the flour and cook 1 to 2 minutes, whisking or stirring continuously, until thickened. Whisk in the port and broth, then the sugar and bring to a boil.

Deglaze the roasting pan by stirring to remove any caramelized bits stuck to the bottom. Season with salt and pepper to taste. Cook about 5 to 10 minutes until thick, then strain through a strainer and serve hot.

Makes about 1¾ cups
Preparation time: 5 minutes, plus making the broth
Cooking time: 15 minutes

meat juices from roasting a chicken
¼ cup all-purpose flour
¼ cup port
2 cups Chicken Broth (see page 197)
1 teaspoon dark brown sugar
sea salt and freshly ground black pepper

Béchamel sauce

Melt the butter in a nonstick pot over low heat. Mix in the flour, using a wooden spoon, and slowly beat together for a few minutes. Remove the pan from the heat and whisk in the milk until blended.

Return to a medium heat, add the studded onion and bring just to a boil, stirring continuously. Turn the heat down to low and simmer about 20 minutes, stirring occasionally to make sure the sauce doesn't stick to the bottom of the pan.

Remove from the heat and strain through a strainer into a clean bowl. Cover with a circle of parchment paper to fit the top of the sauce to stop a skin forming. Let cool.

Store the sauce in an airtight container in the refrigerator for up to 2 days.

Makes 2 cups
Preparation time: 10 minutes
Cooking time: 25 minutes

3½ cups unsalted butter
heaped ⅓ cup all-purpose flour
2 cups warm milk
1 onion studded with 15 cloves

Tomato sauce

Melt the butter in a large pot over medium heat. Add the onion and celery and fry 2 minutes. Add all the remaining ingredients and bring to a boil.

Turn the heat down to low and simmer about 1 hour until rich and thick. Remove and discard the herbs, then let cool.

Store in an airtight container up to a week in the refrigerator.

Makes about 2½ cups
Preparation time: 10 minutes, plus making the broth
Cooking time: 1¼ hours

3½ tablespoons unsalted butter
1 onion, finely chopped
1 celery stick, finely chopped
1 garlic clove, finely chopped
3 tablespoons tomato paste
1¾ cups canned crushed tomatoes
1 thyme sprig
1 rosemary sprig
1¼ cups Chicken or Vegetable Broth (see page 197)
1 bay leaf

Sweet & sour sauce

Heat the peanut oil in a small pot over medium heat. Add the garlic, chili, ginger and pepper and fry 2 to 3 minutes until softened and fragrant. Add the pineapple juice, sugar, ketchup, vinegar, soy sauce and salt. Bring to a boil, then turn the heat down to low and simmer a few minutes, stirring continuously, until the ingredients are well blended and the sugar has dissolved.

In a small bowl, mix the cornstarch to a paste with ¼ cup water, then stir it into the sauce, bring it back to a simmer and cook 1 minute, stirring, until the sauce is smooth and thick. Finally add the sesame oil and stir it into the sauce until blended.

Store in an airtight container up to 3 days in the refrigerator.

Makes about 1½ cups
Preparation time: 5 minutes
Cooking time: 10 minutes

2 tablespoons peanut oil
2 garlic cloves, roughly chopped
½ red chili with seeds, roughly chopped
½-inch piece of ginger root, peeled and
  roughly chopped
2 tablespoons finely chopped red bell
  pepper
¼ cup pineapple juice
¼ cup sugar
2 tablespoons ketchup
2 tablespoons white wine vinegar
1 tablespoon soy sauce
a pinch salt
1½ teaspoons cornstarch
1 tablespoon sesame oil

Hoisin sauce

Put all the ingredients in a large, nonmetallic bowl. Whisk them together until well blended.

Store in an airtight container up to 4 days in the refrigerator.

Serves 4
Preparation time: 5 minutes

¼ cup dark soy sauce
2 tablespoons miso paste
1 tablespoon molasses or honey
1 garlic clove, finely chopped
2 teaspoons sesame oil
1 teaspoon Chinese hot sauce
2 teaspoons rice vinegar
½ teaspoon freshly ground black pepper
1 tablespoon sesame seeds
1 tablespoon oyster sauce

Fresh basil or arugula pesto

Grind the basil or arugula, Parmesan, garlic and nuts to a paste in a small blender or with a mortar and pestle. Gradually beat in the oil until you have a smooth paste. Season with salt and pepper to taste.

Store the pesto in an airtight container in the refrigerator for up to 2 days.

Makes 250ml/9fl ounces/1 cup
Preparation time: 10 minutes

3 cups basil leaves or arugula leaves
⅓ cup shredded parmesan cheese
1 garlic clove
1 tablespoon pine nuts, hazelnuts or
 walnuts
scant ⅔ cup olive oil
sea salt and freshly ground black pepper

Guacamole

Cut the avocados in half, remove the pits, then scoop out the flesh, using a spoon, and put it into a bowl. Add the lime juice and crush with the back of a fork, then add the cilantro and season with salt and pepper to taste.

Serves 4
Preparation time: 10 minutes

2 ripe avocados
juice of ½ lime
1 tablespoon chopped cilantro leaves
1 tablespoon sea salt
1 teaspoon freshly ground black pepper

Tomato salsa

Put all the ingredients in a large bowl. Whisk together until well blended, then season with salt and pepper to taste.

Store in an airtight container up to 2 days in the refrigerator.

Serves 4
Preparation time: 10 minutes

4 large ripe vine tomatoes with seeds,
 finely chopped
½ red onion, finely chopped
2 scallions, thinly sliced
2 tablespoons chopped cilantro leaves
1 tablespoon chopped chives
1 green chili, seeded and finely chopped
sea salt and freshly ground black pepper

Mayonnaise

Whisk together the egg yolks, mustard, vinegar and lemon juice in a nonmetallic bowl until the mixture goes slightly pale and thickens. Gradually drizzle in the oil, a little at a time, whisking continuously until the mayonnaise thickens.

If the mayonnaise is too thick once all the oil is added, whisk in 1 to 2 teaspoons warm water. Season with salt and pepper to taste. If you like, stir in some chopped herbs or spices, according to the recipe.

Store in an airtight container up to 3 days in the refrigerator.

Makes about 1¼ cups
Preparation time: 5 minutes

2 large egg yolks
1 teaspoon Dijon mustard
1 tablespoon white wine vinegar
1 teaspoon lemon juice
1 cup canola oil
sea salt and freshly ground black pepper
1 tablespoon chopped herbs of your choice (optional)
1 teaspoon spice of your choice, such as chili powder or nutmeg (optional)

Tartare sauce

Put all the ingredients in a nonmetallic bowl and whisk together until well blended, seasoning with salt and pepper to taste.

Store in an airtight container up to 3 days in the refrigerator.

Makes about ½ cup
Preparation time: 5 minutes, plus making the mayonnaise

⅓ cup Mayonnaise (see page 202)
2 tablespoons drained capers, rinsed and finely chopped
2 tablespoons chopped gherkins
1 teaspoon chopped parsley leaves
1 teaspoon chopped chives
1 teaspoon chopped dill
1 teaspoon finely chopped shallots
1 teaspoon lemon juice
sea salt and freshly ground black pepper

Bean house salad dressing

Put all the ingredients in a large, nonmetallic bowl. Whisk them together until well blended, then season with salt and pepper to taste.

Store the dressing in an airtight container up to 2 weeks in the refrigerator.

Makes about 2 cups
Preparation time: 5 minutes

1⅓ cups olive oil
⅔ cup white wine vinegar
1 tablespoon Dijon mustard
1 tablespoon wholegrain mustard
3 tablespoons honey
sea salt and freshly ground black pepper

Miso dressing

Put all the ingredients in a nonmetallic bowl and whisk together until well blended, seasoning with salt and pepper to taste.

Store in an airtight container up to a week in the refrigerator.

Makes about 1⅔ cup
Preparation time: 5 minutes

¼ cup light soy sauce
2 tablespoons sesame oil
2 tablespoons mirin
3 to 4 tablespoons miso paste
4 teaspoons white wine vinegar
2 teaspoons honey
sea salt and freshly ground black pepper

Caesar salad dressing

Put all the ingredients in a nonmetallic bowl and whisk together until well blended, seasoning with salt and pepper to taste.

Store in an airtight container up to 3 days in the refrigerator.

Makes about ½ cup
Preparation time: 5 minutes,
    plus making the mayonnaise

½ teaspoon anchovy paste
1 tablespoon white wine vinegar
2 tablespoons Mayonnaise (see page 202)
1 tablespoon Dijon mustard
½ garlic clove, crushed
¼ teaspoon lemon juice
3 tablespoons olive oil
1 tablespoon freshly shredded parmesan
    cheese
sea salt and freshly ground black pepper

Curry paste

Put the seeds and peppercorns in a dry skillet over medium heat and cook about 3 minutes, stirring, until the mustard seeds start to pop and the seeds turn golden and aromatic. Tip into a bowl and let cool a few minutes.

Put the turmeric, cinnamon, paprika and dried chili in a mortar and pestle or spice grinder, add the toasted spices and the salt, and grind together into a fine powder. Add the ginger, garlic, tomato paste and vinegar, and grind or bash to a paste.

Use right away, or spoon the paste into a screw-top jar, top with a little oil and seal with a lid. Keep in an airtight jar up to 2 weeks in the refrigerator.

Makes about 1 cup
Preparation time: 20 minutes
Cooking time: 5 minutes

3 tablespoons coriander seeds
2 tablespoons cumin seeds
1 tablespoon mustard seeds
1 teaspoon fennel seeds
1 teaspoon black peppercorns
1 teaspoon ground turmeric
1 teaspoon ground cinnamon
1 teaspoon paprika
1 dried chili
1 teaspoon salt
1-inch piece of ginger root, peeled and finely grated
4 garlic cloves, finely grated
1 tablespoon tomato paste
¼ cup cider vinegar
a little sunflower oil, to cover the paste while storing

Roasted garlic

Heat the oven to 350°F. Put the garlic in a roasting pan, then drizzle with the oil and bake 10 minutes until golden brown and tender. Let cool.

Store in an airtight container up to 2 weeks in the refrigerator. Squeeze the garlic out of the papery skins when needed.

Makes about 4 ounces
Preparation time: 5 minutes
Cooking time: 10 minutes

6 garlic bulbs, cloves separated but not peeled
⅓ cup oil

Thai curry paste

Put all the ingredients into a small blender and blitz together to a paste, or crush in a mortar and pestle.

Store in an airtight container for up to a week in the refrigerator.

Makes about 1 cup
Preparation time: 15 minutes

3 green chilies, seeded and roughly chopped
3 garlic cloves, crushed
2 tablespoons peeled and finely chopped or grated lemongrass stalks
4 shallots, finely chopped
1 tablespoon peeled and grated ginger root
1 tablespoon finely chopped kaffir lime leaves
2 teaspoons ground coriander
2 teaspoons ground cumin
1 tablespoon Thai fish sauce
1 small bunch of cilantro stalks
2 tablespoons chopped spinach leaves
2 tablespoons olive oil
sea salt and freshly ground black pepper

Crisp fried shallots

Heat ¾ inch of oil in a deep, heavy pot to 325°F, when a cube of bread browns in 60 seconds.

Dip the shallot rings into the milk and make sure all the rings have separated, then dip in the flour, shaking off any excess.

Fry in the hot oil for about 3 minutes until crisp, then drain on paper towels and serve hot.

Serves 4
Preparation time: 10 minutes
Cooking time: 5 minutes

peanut oil, for frying
4 banana shallots, sliced into rings
scant ½ cup milk
heaped ⅓ cup self-rising flour

Spiced apple chutney

Put the apples, onion and ⅓ cup water in a large pot over medium heat and bring to a boil. Turn the heat down to low and simmer 15 minutes until the onion is soft.

Add the salt, spices and half the vinegar, and continue to simmer 10 minutes, stirring occasionally. Add the sugar, syrup and the remaining vinegar, and simmer 5 minutes longer, stirring, until thick and fragrant.

Spoon into airtight jars and leave to finish cooling, then seal and keep for up to 2 months unopened. Once opened, refrigerate and use within 2 to 3 weeks.

Makes about 5 cups
Preparation time: 20 minutes
Cooking time: 35 minutes

1¾ pounds cooking apples, peeled, cored and finely chopped
9 ounces onion, chopped
2 teaspoons sea salt
2 teaspoons ground ginger
½ tablespoon ground cinnamon
¼ teaspoon cayenne pepper
1¼ cups white wine vinegar
1¼ cups dark brown sugar
125g/4½ ounces golden syrup

Mango chutney

Bring all the ingredients to a boil in a large pot over medium heat, then turn the heat down to low and leave to simmer 15 to 20 minutes, stirring occasionally, until rich and thick. Let cool slightly.

Spoon into airtight jars and leave to finish cooling, then seal and keep for up to 2 months. Once opened, refrigerate and use within 2 to 3 weeks.

Makes about 600g/1 pound 5 ounces
Preparation time: 15 minutes
Cooking time: 25 minutes

2 ripe mangoes, peeled, pitted and cut into chunks
1-inch piece of ginger root, peeled and chopped
1 garlic clove, crushed
½ teaspoon mustard seeds
½ teaspoon cumin seeds
¼ red chili, seeded and finely chopped
1½ tablespoons white wine vinegar
⅓ cup white sugar

Fresh egg pasta

Put the flour in a bowl and make a well in the center. Pour the eggs into the well. Gradually whisk the flour into the eggs, a little at a time, then add the oil and start to mix the ingredients together with your hands until you have a soft dough.

Knead and pull the dough for about 3 minutes on a lightly floured surface. Lightly oil a bowl, add the dough, then cover with plastic wrap and put in the refrigerator for at least 30 minutes.

Roll out the dough on a floured surface as thinly as you can, or use a pasta machine. Use to make ravioli, fettucine, linguine or other pasta shapes.

Makes about 1 pound
Preparation time: 15 minutes,
  plus 30 minutes resting

3 cups pasta flour, plus extra for dusting
4 eggs, beaten with a pinch salt
1 tablespoon olive oil, plus extra for
  greasing

Pizza dough

Mix together the flour and salt in a bowl. In another bowl, add the yeast to 1⅓ cups warm water, leave for 1 minute, then stir until dissolved. Pour the mixture into the flour and bring together to a smooth, slightly tacky dough.

Turn the dough onto a lightly floured surface and knead for about 2 minutes until the dough is smooth and no longer sticky.

Put the dough in an oiled bowl, cover with plastic wrap and leave in a warm, not hot, place for 1 hour to rise.

Turn the dough out onto a lightly floured surface, punch down the dough, using your fist, then knead again for a few minutes.

Use as directed in the recipe, or split and roll the dough into pizza bases. For a thin base, roll as thinly as you can, put on a baking sheet, add the topping and bake right away in a heated oven at 425°F for about 8 minutes. For a thicker base, don't roll out as much, put on a baking sheet and add the topping, then cover loosely with plastic wrap and leave in a warm place 10 minutes to prove before baking.

Makes about 1 pound 9 ounces
Preparation time: 15 minutes,
  plus 1 hour rising
Cooking time: 10 minutes

4 cups strong white bread flour,
  plus extra for dusting
2 teaspoons salt
2 teaspoons fresh yeast or 1½ teaspoons
  dried yeast
a little oil, for greasing

Rough puff pastry dough

Mix together the flour and salt in a bowl, then make a well in the center and add the butter. Rub in the butter, using your fingertips, until the butter is broken up but still visible in lumps.

Gradually add the cold water, a drop at a time, to bind the ingredients together, but don't overwork the dough as you still want to be able to see the lumps of butter. Wrap in plastic wrap and chill 20 to 30 minutes in the refrigerator.

Roll out the dough on a lightly floured surface into a rectangle about 16 x 8 inches with the long side facing you. Fold over one-third of the pastry from each side to make a 5- x 8-inch rectangle, then give it a quarter turn. Repeat this three times, then wrap and chill again for 30 minutes. (If the dough gets too warm, chill 30 minutes in the refrigerator before finishing the folds.)

Makes about 1 pound
Preparation time: 30 minutes,
 plus 1½ hours chilling

1¾ cups all-purpose flour, plus extra
 for dusting
1 teaspoon salt
1 cup very cold unsalted butter, cubed
½ cup cold water

Pastry dough

Put the flour in a large bowl, then rub in the butter, using your fingertips, until the mixture resembles coarse breadcrumbs.

Make a well in the center and add the egg, then bring the mixture together with your hands, gradually adding 1 to 2 tablespoons water, if necessary, to bind the mixture into a dough.

Turn out onto a cold, lightly floured surface and knead gently until fully mixed. Wrap in plastic wrap and chill at least 10 minutes in the refrigerator before using.

Makes ½ pound
Preparation time: 10 minutes,
 plus at least 10 minutes chilling

2 cups all-purpose flour, plus extra
 for dusting
½ cup cold unsalted butter, cubed
1 egg

Anchovy straws

Heat the oven to 350°F and line a baking sheet with parchment paper.

Lay the dough on a lightly floured surface and cut into ½-inch strips, then spread the anchovy paste over the dough. Holding each end of one strip, slowly twist it all the way along, then put it on the prepared baking sheet. Repeat with the remaining dough strips.

Bake 8 to 10 minutes until golden brown. Serve warm or cold.

Serves 4
Preparation time: 10 minutes
Cooking time: 10 minutes

9 ounces ready-rolled puff pastry
a little flour, for dusting
2 tablespoons anchovy paste

Smoked paprika wraps

Mix together the flour, smoked paprika , salt, pepper and baking powder in a bowl. Add the butter and rub together until the mixture resembles breadcrumbs. Gradually add 1¾ cups boiling water, mixing with a wooden spoon and gradually bringing the ingredients together to form a soft dough.

Knead the dough on a lightly floured surface 2 minutes until smooth, then put in an oiled bowl, cover with plastic wrap and leave 10 minutes. Divide the dough into 12 equal portions, roll into balls and keep covered.

Put a piece of parchment paper on the counter and dust with flour. Put the first portion of dough on the paper, sprinkle with flour and lay another piece on top. Roll out the dough thinly between the sheets, turning every roll to keep an even shape. Repeat with the rest of the dough.

Heat a large, dry skillet over high heat. Add the first wrap and cook about 30 seconds on each side until just browned. Remove from the pan and let cool.

Use right away or store in an airtight container up to 2 days in the refrigerator or freeze for up to a month.

Serves 4
Preparation time: 20 minutes,
   plus 1 hour rising
Cooking time: 12 minutes

3 cups all-purpose flour, plus extra
   for dusting
1 tablespoon smoked paprika
1 teaspoon salt
1 teaspoon freshly ground black pepper
1 teaspoon baking powder
2 tablespoons unsalted butter, cubed
a little oil, for greasing

accompaniments

Spiced rice & lentils

Soak the lentils in cold water for 1 hour, then drain well.

Heat the oil and butter in a large pot. Add the onion and fry 1 minute, stirring. Add all the spices and fry 2 minutes longer.

Drain the lentils, then add them to the pot and cook, stirring, for 2 minutes longer. Add the broth and cilantro, season with salt and pepper and bring to a boil. Turn the heat down to low, cover with a lid and simmer 10 minutes.

Remove from the heat and let stand, covered, 5 minutes, then stir well before serving.

Serves 4
Preparation time: 10 minutes, plus 1 hour soaking, and making the broth
Cooking time: 25 minutes

$\frac{1}{2}$ cup red split lentils
2 tablespoons vegetable oil
$3\frac{1}{2}$ ounces unsalted butter
1 onion, thinly sliced
1 cinnamon stick
2 cardamom pods
2 cloves
1 red chili
1 tablespoon cumin seeds
1 teaspoon ground turmeric
generous 2 cups Vegetable Broth
  (see page 197)
$\frac{1}{3}$ cup finely chopped cilantro leaves
$1\frac{1}{3}$ cups basmati rice
sea salt and freshly ground black pepper

Saffron rice

Heat the oil and butter in a large pot over medium-high heat. Add the cardamom pods, cinnamon sticks and cumin seeds and fry 30 seconds.

Add the rice, and stir until coated in the butter and oil, then stir in the saffron. Add $4\frac{1}{3}$ cups water and the salt and bring to a boil. Turn the heat down to low, cover with a lid and simmer gently 8 to 10 minutes until the rice is tender and the water is absorbed.

Stir the lemon zest through the rice and serve.

Serves 4
Preparation time: 5 minutes
Cooking time: 15 minutes

2 tablespoons olive oil
2 tablespoons unsalted butter
4 cardamom pods
2 cinnamon sticks
1 teaspoon cumin seeds
3 cups basmati rice, rinsed
a large pinch of saffron strands
$\frac{1}{2}$ teaspoon sea salt
grated zest of 2 lemons

Mediterranean vegetable couscous

Put the couscous in a large, heavy pot over medium heat and cook about 5 minutes, shaking the pan frequently and stirring to keep the grains moving around the pan, until the couscous is a lovely mottled, toasted color. Immediately remove from the heat and tip into a bowl. If you leave it in the pan, it can burn very quickly.

Bring the broth to a boil in a pot over high heat. Pour over the couscous and stir well. Cover with plastic wrap and leave 10 to 15 minutes until the couscous is tender and has absorbed most of the liquid, stirring occasionally. Drain off any excess liquid.

Put the peppers and zucchini in a bowl, drizzle with the oil and toss together, then add them to the couscous along with the herbs, lemon zest and juice. Season with salt and pepper to taste, then mix together.

Serves 4
Preparation time: 10 minutes, plus 20 minutes standing, and making the broth
Cooking time: 10 minutes

heaped 1 cup couscous
scant 1¼ cups Vegetable Broth (see page 197)
1 red bell pepper, seeded and finely chopped
1 yellow bell pepper, seeded and finely chopped
1 zucchini, finely chopped
2 tablespoons olive oil
2 tablespoons chopped parsley leaves
1 tablespoon chopped mint leaves
grated zest and juice of ½ lemon
sea salt and freshly ground black pepper

Ratatouille

Heat the oil in a large pot over medium heat. Add all the vegetables and the thyme and cook about 2 minutes.

Add the broth, tomatoes and tomato paste, bring to a boil, then turn the heat down to low and simmer about 10 minutes. Stir in the pesto and season with a little salt and pepper to taste.

Serve right away or store up to 3 days in the refrigerator and reheat in a pot when needed.

Serves 4
Preparation time: 20 minutes, plus making the broth and pesto
Cooking time: 30 minutes

2 tablespoons olive oil
1 onion, finely chopped
1 red bell pepper, seeded and chopped
1 yellow bell pepper, seeded and chopped
½ eggplant, cut into ¾-inch cubes
1 zucchini, cut into ¾-inch cubes
1 teaspoon thyme leaves
1¼ cups Vegetable Broth (see page 197)
1¾ cups canned crushed tomatoes
1 tablespoon tomato paste
1 tablespoon Fresh Basil Pesto (see page 201)
sea salt and freshly ground black pepper

Creamy mashed potatoes

Bring a large pot of lightly salted water to a boil over high heat, add the potatoes and boil 15 to 20 minutes until tender, then drain well and return to the pan. Cover and set aside to dry for 5 minutes, then mash with a potato masher or put the potato through a potato ricer.

Put the cream, butter and thyme in a small pot over medium heat and bring to a boil. Remove from the heat, discard the thyme and pour the cream into the mash. Season with salt and pepper and bind together with a wooden spoon until well blended. Serve immediately or cool, cover and store in the refrigerator for up to 3 days.

Serves 4
Preparation time: 10 minutes
Cooking time: 25 minutes

1 pound baking potatoes, peeled and chopped
1 cup heavy cream
3 tablespoons unsalted butter
1 thyme sprig
sea salt and freshly ground black pepper

Roast potatoes

Put the potatoes in a pot and rinse under cold water until the water runs completely clear. This will remove much of the starch from the potatoes. Drain, then fill the pot with cold water to cover the potatoes. Bring to a boil over high heat, then turn the heat down to medium and simmer about 5 to 10 minutes until the potatoes are just tender in the center but not fully cooked.

Drain into a colander, then shake the colander to roughen the edges of the potatoes. Let them air dry for at least 5 minutes. Cover and chill at least 1 hour or overnight in the refrigerator.

Heat the oven to 350°F. Heat the oil and fat in a large, flameproof roasting pan, then carefully add the potatoes one at a time. Cook on the stove for about 5 minutes, turning with a set of tongs until browned on all sides. Add the thyme and garlic, transfer to the oven and roast 25 minutes. Turn and move the potatoes around, then return them to the oven 20 minutes longer until golden and crisp. Drain well before serving.

Serves 4
Preparation time: 10 minutes, plus at least 1 hour drying and chilling
Cooking time: 1 hour

2¼ pounds good-quality baking potatoes, peeled and cut into even-size 2-inch pieces
¾ cup olive oil
½ cup duck or goose fat
2 thyme sprigs
2 garlic cloves, crushed

French fries

Put the prepared potatoes in a colander, and the colander in a bowl of cold water and let stand for 10 minutes. Rinse in cold water until the water runs clear to remove the starch and help the fries stay crisp. Leave in cold, fresh water.

Heat a deep, heavy pot of oil to 300°F, when a cube of day-old bread browns in 80 seconds. Line a baking sheet with paper towels. Drain the fries and pat dry on a clean cloth. Gently lower about one-quarter of the french fries into the hot oil, so the pan is not too full, and cook 2 to 3 minutes until they are soft in the center. Carefully lift one out on a slotted spoon and pinch it to check. Lift the fries out of the oil onto the prepared baking sheet. Cook the remaining fries, then put them in the refrigerator, uncovered, 10 minutes to chill.

To finish the fries, increase the oil temperature to 350°F, or when a cube of bread browns in 60 seconds. Add the § fries in batches and fry about 2 minutes until golden and crisp. Remove from the oil, shake dry, then season with a little salt.

Serves 4
Preparation time: 20 minutes, plus 20 minutes standing and chilling
Cooking time: 20 minutes

4 large baking potatoes, peeled and cut into even-size french fries
peanut oil, for deep-frying
sea salt

Potato Dauphinoise

Heat the oven to 350°F and butter a small ovenproof dish. Peel the potatoes, then cut them into ¼-inch slices using a mandoline. Put in a bowl and cover with cold water to prevent them from discoloring. Warm the cream, onion, garlic and thyme in a small pot.

Drain the potato slices and start to layer them in the bottom of the prepared dish, overlapping the edges of the potatoes, seasoning every couple of layers with salt and pepper. Continue until the dish is three-quarters full.

Slowly pour the garlic and thyme cream over the potatoes, letting it drain through the layers. Sprinkle the shredded cheese on top, then bake in the oven for 20 to 30 minutes until golden in color and the potatoes are tender.

Serves 4
Preparation time: 15 minutes
Cooking time: 35 minutes

a little butter, for greasing
1 pound baking potatoes
1 cup heavy cream
½ onion, thinly sliced
1 garlic clove, finely chopped
1 teaspoon chopped thyme leaves
⅓ cup sharp shredded cheddar cheese
sea salt and freshly ground black pepper

Potato croquettes

Heat the oven to 315°F. Put the cold mashed potatoes in a bowl. If you like, mix in your chosen flavoring to taste. Put the breadcrumbs in a shallow bowl. Whisk together the eggs and milk in another shallow bowl with a pinch of salt to make an egg wash.

Heat 1½ inches of oil in a deep, heavy skillet to 350°F, when a cube of bread browns in 50 seconds.

Take a tablespoonful of the mashed potato at a time and roll into a ball. Dip the potato balls in the egg wash, shake off any excess, then roll in the breadcrumbs.

Add the croquettes to the hot oil a few at a time and fry about 3 minutes until heated through and browned on all sides. Lift out of the pan, using a slotted spoon, drain on paper towels, then put in the oven to keep warm until you have fried the remaining croquettes.

Serves 4
Preparation time: 20 minutes,
 plus making the mash
Cooking time: 15 minutes

1 recipe quantity Creamy Mashed Potatoes
 (see page 212), chilled
flavorings, such as cooked smoked bacon,
 mustard, 1 tablespoon chopped chives,
 tarragon or other herbs (optional)
1 cup panko breadcrumbs
2 eggs
2 tablespoons milk
olive oil, for frying
sea salt and freshly ground black pepper

Parmentier potatoes

Trim the sides of the potatoes to make them square, then cut into ½-inch slices. Cut the slices into ½-inch strips, then the strips into ½-inch cubes. Rinse under cold water to remove the excess starch.

Heat the peanut oil in a deep, heavy pot to 325°F, when a cube of bread browns in 60 seconds. Add the potatoes and fry about 5 minutes until golden. Drain on paper towels, season well with salt and pepper and serve.

Serves 4
Preparation time: 10 minutes
Cooking time: 10 minutes

1¼ pounds baking potatoes, peeled
peanut oil, for deep-frying
sea salt and freshly ground black pepper

Sweet potato wedges

Heat the oven to 400°F.

Put the sweet potato wedges on a baking sheet, skin-side down, drizzle with the oil, sprinkle with the smoked paprika and season with a little salt and pepper. Bake 20 to 30 minutes until crisp on the outside and slightly soft in the center. Serve hot.

Serves 4
Preparation time: 4 minutes
Cooking time: 30 minutes

4 sweet potatoes, cut into wedges
   lengthwise
3 tablespoons olive oil
½ teaspoon smoked paprika
sea salt and freshly ground black pepper

Sweet potato or parsnip crisps

Using a vegetable peeler, cut thin strips off the sweet potatoes or parsnips, from top to bottom, while turning the vegetable so you are peeling it evenly into long strips.

Heat the oil in a deep, heavy pot to 315°F, when a cube of bread browns in 70 seconds. Using a slotted spoon, gently lower a spoonful of the vegetable strips into the hot oil and cook 2 to 3 minutes, gently turning them in the oil until they are evenly golden in color. Lift out of the pot, using a slotted spoon, and drain on paper towels. Continue to fry the remaining vegetables. Season with salt and pepper to taste.

Serve sprinkled on any chicken dish or just as a tasty snack.

Serves 4
Preparation time: 10 minutes
Cooking time: 10 minutes

2 sweet potatoes or 4 parsnips, peeled
1⅔ cups peanut oil
sea salt and freshly ground black pepper

Honey-roasted root vegetables

Heat the oven to 400°F. Bring a pot of water to a boil over high heat, add the parsnips, carrots and celery root and boil 4 minutes until just soft in the middle. Drain and refresh under cold water to stop them cooking any further, then drain again. Put in a roasting tray and season with salt and pepper.

Whisk together the honey and mustard, then drizzle it over the vegetables and roast 15 to 20 minutes until golden in color, shaking halfway through to coat the vegetables in the honey and mustard.

Serves 4
Preparation time: 15 minutes
Cooking time: 30 minutes

2 parsnips, cut into sticks
3 carrots, cut into sticks
7 ounces celery root, cut into sticks
   (about 2 cups)
2 tablespoons honey
1 tablespoon Dijon mustard
1 teaspoon chopped thyme leaves
sea salt and freshly ground black pepper

Buttered carrots

Bring a pot of water to a boil over high heat. Add the carrots and cook 2 minutes, then run under cold water until cold, or put into a bowl of ice-cold water to stop them cooking any further. Drain, then return to the pot.

Add the butter and parsley to the carrots and put the pot over medium heat. Cook in the pot for 3 to 4 minutes until the carrots are hot and covered in the herb butter. Serve right away or cool and reheat when needed.

Serves 4
Preparation time: 5 minutes
Cooking time: 10 minutes

14 ounces small carrots, cut in half
   lengthwise, or larger carrots, quartered
   or cut into chunks
1 tablespoon unsalted butter
2 tablespoons chopped parsley leaves

Golden onions

Heat the oil in a pot over medium heat. Add the onions and fry quickly for 1 to 2 minutes until light golden in color.

Add enough water to come halfway up the onions and stir in the sugar. Heat, stirring, until the sugar has melted, then bring to a boil. Turn the heat down to low and simmer about 15 minutes until the onions are just tender and the liquid has reduced to a syrup.

Serves 4
Preparation time: 5 minutes
Cooking time: 20 minutes

3 tablespoons olive oil
2 cups pearl onions, peeled
¼ cup sugar

Wilted greens

Bring a pot of water to a boil over high heat. Add the cabbage and cook 2 minutes, then drain and put into a bowl of ice-cold water to stop it from cooking any further. Drain well.

Melt the butter in a pot over medium heat. Add the drained cabbage and stir for 1 to 2 minutes, then add the spinach and stir for 3 to 4 minutes until the spinach has softened and is warm. Season with a little salt and pepper to taste. Serve right from the pan.

Serves 4
Preparation time: 5 minutes
Cooking time: 10 minutes

½ Savoy cabbage, thinly sliced
2 tablespoons unsalted butter
4 cups spinach leaves
sea salt and freshly ground black pepper

Celery root rémoulade

Mix together the celery root and lemon juice in a nonmetallic bowl. Stir in all the remaining ingredients and season with salt and pepper to taste. Serve right from the bowl.

Serves 4
Preparation time: 10 minutes,
   plus making the mayonnaise

14 ounces celery root, peeled and grated
   into long strips (about 4 cups)
juice of ½ lemon
⅓ cup Mayonnaise (see page 202)
3 tablespoons drained capers, rinsed and
   finely chopped
2 tablespoons chopped parsley leaves
1 tablespoon chopped chives
1 tablespoon heavy cream

Slow-roasted tomatoes

Heat the oven to the lowest possible heat, 200°F. Slice the tomatoes right down the center, then cut each half into wedges, making sure all the wedges are the same size. Put on a baking sheet, skin-side down. Drizzle with a little of the olive oil, then sprinkle with the salt, garlic and thyme leaves.

Roast 4 to 6 hours until dried but still slightly flexible, checking every hour since you don't want them to dry completely. Let cool.

Spoon into a screw-top jar and cover with the remaining oil. Store up to a month in the refrigerator.

Makes about 2 cups
Preparation time: 10 minutes
Cooking time: 6 hours

12 large vine tomatoes
½ cup olive oil
2 tablespoons sea salt crystals
3 garlic cloves, roughly chopped
leaves from 3 thyme sprigs

Celery root & carrot coleslaw

Put the celery root, carrot and onion in a bowl and toss together.

Mix the mayonnaise with the mustard and lemon juice, and season with salt and pepper to taste. Serve at once, or transfer to an airtight container and store up to 3 days in the refrigerator.

Serves 4
Preparation time: 15 minutes,
   plus making the mayonnaise

1 cup peeled and finely grated celery root
1 cup peeled and finely grated carrots
¼ cup thinly sliced onion
3 to 4 tablespoons Mayonnaise
   (see page 202)
2 teaspoons Dijon mustard (optional)
1 teaspoon lemon juice
sea salt and freshly ground black pepper

Green salad

Put all the ingredients in a bowl, then drizzle the salad dressing over them, season with salt and pepper and toss gently to combine. Serve immediately.

Serves 4
Preparation time: 10 minutes

4 scallions, diagonally sliced
1 small romaine lettuce, thinly sliced
½ English cucumber, sliced lengthwise
  then cut into thin strips
2 cups baby spinach leaves, chopped
1 small handful snow peas, thinly sliced
1 tablespoon Bean House Salad Dressing
  (see page 203)

Herb salad

Put all the herbs in a bowl, sprinkle the sesame seeds over the top, then drizzle the salad dressing over them and toss gently to combine. Serve immediately.

Serves 4
Preparation time: 10 minutes

1¼ cups flat-leaf parsley leaves, chopped
1¼ cups cilantro leaves, roughly chopped
2 tablespoons chopped chives
2 cups arugula or watercress leaves
1¼ cups mint leaves, roughly chopped
1 cup basil leaves, roughly torn
3 tablespoons toasted sesame seeds
1 to 2 tablespoons Bean House Salad
  Dressing (see page 203)

Microleaf & carrot salad

Put all the ingredients together in a bowl, then drizzle the dressing over the salad and toss together gently. Serve immediately.

Serves 4
Preparation time: 10 minutes

1¾ cups tenderstem pea shoots
1¼ cups borage leaves
1¼ cups garlic chives, chopped
2 cups micro watercress
1¼ cups micro cilantro
1¼ cups micro red vein sorrel
¼ cup finely grated carrot
1 to 2 tablespoons Bean House Salad
  Dressing (see page 203)

index

acknowledgements

A big thanks to Grace Cheetham for asking me to write this book. I have to admit it was a lot harder than I first thought, but I got there in the end. Thanks, Grace, Rebecca, Wendy and the team, for bearing with me.

An enormous vote of thanks has to go to my wife, Jenny, and our daughters, Ella and Ava, for supporting me while I've been working all day and through the night testing recipes and typing.

A big thank you to my butcher—John Sykes from Shrewsbury market—for supplying me with lots of chicken.

Thanks to Dave Parker, a good friend and top chef, for helping me develop and test some of the recipes.

I hope everyone likes it and that in some way it helps you all on your own culinary journey.

NOURISH
EAT WELL. LIVE WELL

We hope you've enjoyed this Nourish book. Here at Nourish we're all about wellbeing through food and drink—irresistible dishes with a serious good-for-you factor. If you want to eat and drink delicious things that set you up for the day, suit any special diets, keep you healthy and make the most of what you can afford, we've got some great ideas to share with you. Come over to our blog for wholesome recipes and fresh inspiration—nourishbooks.com.